THE HAPPY
MOM MINDSET

*7 Ways to Skip the Mom Traps So You Can Think,
Feel, and Be Happy*

Molly Claire

ISBN-13: 978-1548104993

ISBN-10:154810499X

For bulk purchase and for booking, contact:

molly@mollyclaire.com
www.mollyclaire.com

TABLE OF CONTENTS

9.18.18

INTRODUCTION

This isn't a parenting book.

It's not a book of advice either.

It's not a laundry list of things you "should" be doing.

I don't think you need more parenting advice, more pressure, or another guilt trip.

What you really need is to feel empowered.

You need to find that magical place inside of you that knows exactly what you're doing. You need to feel confident and capable as a mom and comfortable in your own skin. You need to feel successful and fulfilled.

And so, I wrote this book for you.

Because *you* are remarkable.

All the hours you spend doing "invisible" work for everyone around you is not invisible at all. Just because no one notices today doesn't mean it doesn't matter tomorrow.

I know inside, you worry that you're not doing enough, but that's just because you have such big plans. You are a visionary and a creator of miracles. Of course you think you're not measuring up, because *you're not yet where you plan to be.*

You're on your way. One step, one mistake, and one success at a time. It's all part of the plan.

There's no need to do a lifetime of work in a day. Trust me, you're right on track.

I know sometimes you worry you're doing it all wrong, but that's not true either. Remember, you're charting new territory. You can't know what you're doing until you've done it. Be patient with yourself even when it feels impossible to do.

You've made a lot of mistakes, and you'll make a lot more. This is great news. You're trying, and growing, and not giving up. Those mistakes are there to teach you and move you to the next level. You can use every single one of them as leverage. There's no need to use them against yourself; you deserve so much better.

You're on a powerful journey, and journeys take time—especially one this incredible. When the journey is hard, you might cry or lose your temper. You'll question your decisions and feel remorse for each of the million and one mistakes that you make. Despite all of this, keep putting one foot in front of the other.

The way you give and love every day is more powerful than you can imagine.

You're a mom, a partner, a friend, and a woman whose value is beyond measure.

And it's so much more than just what you do... it's who you are.

You are loved. You are valued. Yes, you are remarkable.

And here is your book....

EXPECTATIONS

As you begin this book, you want to know what to expect. What's the format? How can it help me? You want a basic idea of what type of book this really is.

As I set the stage for you here, I find it incredibly ironic that we're starting with expectations. After all, when it comes to motherhood… *it's never what you expect.* Every time you figure one thing out, something else comes along. A good motto for motherhood could be: "Relax, nothing is under control."

When I entered the world of adulthood, I thought I knew what to expect. I thought I knew what I wanted and how to make it happen. College, career, marriage, kids, happily ever after. For me, family life was the most important of my goals. I wanted to create for my family what I wished I'd had as a kid. I wanted a great marriage with plenty of time and energy to raise my kids, plus a life that kept me fulfilled. I was committed to living my life in a way that would *ensure* success and happiness. I charted a path to get from point A to point B. I thought it would be a straight-ish line.

I soon found that "grown-up" life didn't exactly look like a straight line, and motherhood was no exception.

Becoming a mom was not what I expected. Of course, in many ways, it was more than I could have ever imagined. Indescribable and magical, for sure.

But when it came to "doing" motherhood... *I wasn't sure I was making the cut.*

When I became a mom, my son didn't follow the "rules" in the baby advice books. He had colic, allergies, asthma, ear infections, rashes... and I lived with chronic migraines. How could my son have every complication known to man? And how could I be so bad at something I was sure that I was meant to do?

My second son followed suit. Unexpectedly, he was a great sleeper (thank goodness...), but he also had anaphylactic allergies, surgery at age two, and high levels of anxiety in the preschool years when every other kid was only worried about getting a snack.

I found myself becoming worried and uptight.

None of this was what I expected.

And my third... well, you're a mom... you get it. Just when you think you've got it figured out, it all changes. Yes, I had a *girl*! I felt like I was back to square one, and square one was nowhere near the Point B I had been aiming for.

What I really didn't expect was so much fear around how my kids would turn out. I didn't know how intense the fear of failure could be until I was responsible for raising another human being. I could never have anticipated the weight on my shoulders or the doubt that would be woven throughout every decision along the way. I didn't know how extremely aware I would become of my own shortcomings until I expected something so great of myself. It was all so very unexpected.

And so I write this book for you to help you to navigate the unexpected.

Because after years of believing that I needed to have my life and my circumstances a certain way in order to feel happy, accomplished, and satisfied, I learned something magical, and I want to share it with you.

I learned how my current experience—of stress, or worry, or inade-quacy—was a direct result of what was happening inside my brain. It wasn't my kids, or my husband, or my friends who were "making" me feel anything.

I finally understood what Dale Carnegie really meant when he said, "Remember, happiness doesn't depend upon who you are or what you have; ***it depends solely on what you think.***"

And so I'm here to teach you the same thing.

And here's what you can *expect…*

My goal with this book is to teach you the common "Mom Traps" that most of us fall into in one way or another. These traps (which are really brain traps) are the reasons you are feeling stressed, overwhelmed, worried, and frustrated. The traps will also leave you feeling unfulfilled and dissatisfied, with no sense of who you are separate from "mom." They're also the reason you often feel like a failure. They create a less-than-happy experience of motherhood (and you deserve better).

The basic premise of this work is the idea that our thoughts create our feelings, which drive our actions and create our results. It's a universal truth put in a very simple way that's easy to apply and understand. I didn't make this up, nor did anyone else that claims to. It just is. It has been studied and described by many different people in many different ways, but the concept is just the way the universe works.

The way we think creates our experience of life.

I'm going to teach you how to change your experience of moth-erhood and every other aspect of your life simply by looking at your thought patterns and what they are creating for you.

I'm not teaching "positive thinking." My intention is to actually help you take a look at the way your brain works and understand how that plays out in your life and relationships. I know it sounds a bit complicated, but it's as simple as this:

Let's say you've tried to lose weight in the past, without success.

You think: I'll never lose weight.

You feel: Hopeless.

And so you: Turn on Netflix and binge on ice cream.

As a result: You don't lose weight (and maybe gain a bit more).

That's it. A perfect example of our thoughts or beliefs playing out to create the exact result we believe will happen.

Let's look at another one.

Your son's room is a huge mess even though you told him to clean it.

You think: He never listens to me.

You feel: Angry.

And so you: Yell at him to clean up his room now.

As a result: He probably tunes you out halfway through the lecture. He doesn't want to hear it.

As you can see, the end result of this is that he's not listening to you. Your thoughts created a feeling, which drove your actions, which created a result. And that result proved your original thought. Like magic.

This exact sequence is happening all day, every day, in every aspect of our lives. This may seem deep and complicated, but I'm here to make it simple.

Going forward, I'll simply refer to it as "the model," as described by Brooke Castillo.

The model is this:

> C: Circumstance (things outside of your control)
>
> T: Thought (the thought you have about the circumstance)
>
> F: Feeling (the feeling the thought creates for you)
>
> A: Action (the action you take when you have that feeling)
>
> R: Result (the result created by your action, which proves the original thought)

Using this model over and over will help you begin to apply it in your own life. You will start to be aware of all the results you are creating—good and bad. As you do, you'll begin to understand that *you have the power to actually change your experiences.*

Up to this point, you've probably focused on merely changing your actions in order to get a different result. Perhaps you've said, "I need to stop watching Netflix and eating ice cream," or, "I need to stop yelling at my son."

You are so focused on the actions you want to change (and feeling terrible that you haven't done it yet) that you're missing out on understanding the thoughts and beliefs that caused you to gain weight or yell in the first place.

You think you are yelling because you're a crappy mom or you have no patience, but you're not.

Or maybe you think you are yelling because his room isn't clean, but you're not.

The only reason you are yelling is that you are having a thought that he never listens to you (which you may interpret as him not respecting you), which causes you to feel angry. That anger is driving the action and creating the result.

As women, we are so hard on ourselves and spend way too much time beating ourselves up for not taking better action or creating a different result. But beating yourself up or putting yourself down is not necessary (nor is it useful).

I'm going to teach you how to stop the negative self-talk, the shame, and the ineffective blame you are putting on yourself. I'm here to help you move away from feeling bad about unwanted actions and teach you how to actually make the changes you want to make.

I'm here to help you create a completely different experience of raising a child with disabilities.

I'm here to help you find hope and solutions when it comes to the power struggles you can't seem to get out of.

I'm here to help you finally create that fulfillment and peace of mind that you so desperately want in your life and relationships. It begins and ends in your mind—so let's learn how to make it happen.

Throughout the book, I'll give specific client examples (all names and some details have been changed). I want to give you a taste of what's possible as you learn and apply this work.

The constant pressure you feel does not need to be the norm. When you feel pressure, you are ineffective and unhappy. I believe in being productive, amazing, and making a huge difference in the world by creating powerful feelings that drive positive action. You don't need to feel pressure in order to change the world. What you need is hope, confidence, and empowerment.

And what about guilt? Ah yes, the nagging, bring-you-down, ineffective kind—it's not necessary. There's a difference between useful guilt that helps us to improve and the empty guilt that simply swirls in our brains and ruins our days. That constant chatter in your head is cluttering up your brain and your life. Let's call it what it is and clear it out.

We're ready to dive into the traps!

A quick preview of what's to come:

Trap 1 and **Trap 2** contain a lot of practical, nitty-gritty, hands-on stuff. There will be some "take action" ideas and a lot of information. Take what applies to you and leave the rest. You're not supposed to do it all or learn it all. The idea is that as you learn about the traps, you will experience automatic shifts in your thought processes. Raising your awareness is the best gift I can give you.

Trap 3 might be my favorite chapter. Starting with this chapter, it's much less "practical" but aimed at addressing some of the real issues going on for you underneath the surface. Feeling like a failure or that you aren't doing enough are a couple of big ones.

Twin chapters **Trap 4** and **Trap 5** will help you untangle your success and happiness from your kids. Here, we will dig even further into the the thought model and understand it at a new level.

Trap 6 is smaller in size, but huge in it's impact. It addresses one common thought pattern and how it's smothering your joy and sense of freedom.

Trap 7 is all about you. I left it until the end because I want to make sure you remember it. It's one of my biggest lessons in life, and I'm excited to share it with you.

The Workbook—is a must! It's for the hands-on application of everything I'm teaching you here. It's loaded with questions and exercises to help you implement the concepts and change your life. You can access it on my website at www.mollyclaire.com/HappyMomMindsetWorkbook.

WHAT ABOUT WHEN... CHALLENGES YOU'LL FACE

The strategies I'm going to teach you are simple enough, but there's no doubt that you'll face some challenges when you get started. Remember, the most powerful thing I can offer you in this book is a raised awareness of your thought patterns and what they are currently creating for you. The way you think about your life creates your experience of your life.

Use the workbook to help you work through this book on a personal level. Revisit this book often, and use the strategies here to constantly raise your awareness of the thoughts in your head. You can't know what needs to change until you know what's really happening.

Once your awareness has been raised, there are a couple common challenges to implementing the solutions. Let's talk about them…

Consistency

Many of us struggle with consistency and believe that we're not able to make changes because we can't be consistent. This can get in the way of us even getting started with new ideas like those I'm going to share with you in this book. It's easy to think, "I can't be consistent." We often look at the ways we haven't been consistent or followed through in the past and use it as evidence that we won't do it this time either.

This type of thinking is not useful for you at all. So what if you weren't consistent on the last commitment you made? It doesn't have to mean that you aren't capable of doing it this time. Being consistent is a practice. The more you practice being consistent, the more consistent you will be. And when you don't follow through, you can choose to be curious about why and figure out what needs to change rather than using it as a reason to believe that you can never be consistent.

If you want to be consistent in implementing one of the solutions here, make a small commitment and follow through on it. You can ask yourself the question, "How can I create evidence that I can be consistent?" This is a great question to pique your curiosity while empowering you to create exactly what you want. The only thing in the way of you being consistent is your thinking, and what you choose to think is completely optional.

"We are what we repeatedly do. Excellence then, is not an act, but a habit." –Aristotle

Resistance

You may find yourself experiencing some resistance to the suggestions I make in the coming chapters. Maybe that's okay. Maybe you don't want to do everything I share with you, or maybe you aren't ready. When my clients have resistance to something, we always find out why, but I never fight against the resistance.

Instead, I encourage my clients to continue to raise their awareness and ask themselves what they want and what's best for them. I invite you to do the same. Raising your awareness will guide you to make the best decisions for yourself. If you try to push through the resistance, you'll simply end up in a power struggle with this book. Instead, find out what you are resistant to and why. As a result, you can also find out what you want and what might be the best way to get you there.

THE RULE (Yes, I've got a rule.)

Read this book your way. If something isn't what you need or want, move on to a chapter that's more useful. Don't get caught up in "doing it right." Your way is the right way.

And so, let's begin!

The Workbook—is a must! It's for the hands-on application of everything I'm teaching you here. It's loaded with questions and exercises to help you implement the concepts and change your life. You can access it on my website at www.mollyclaire.com/HappyMomMindsetWorkbook.

TRAP 1

MOM AUTOPILOT: FULL SPEED AHEAD

THE TRUTH:
You are an individual with a great and mighty purpose. All the joy and life satisfaction you crave is available to you. If you feel frustrated or stuck in your life, perhaps you need to turn off autopilot and get intentional about your flight path.

"Live less out of habit, and more out of intent." –Unknown

THE TRAP: MOM AUTOPILOT

As we dive into learning about the first Mom Trap, you'll discover that you are taking on more than you want to without realizing it. I don't just mean physical tasks, but also taking on more stress and worry than is necessary. This is all *good* news. It means something better is just around the corner. This trap is not exclusive to any one phase of life, or even motherhood, for that matter. Whether you have toddlers, teenagers, or just feel caught in the daily grind of life—this chapter is for you.

Let's get some fresh perspective and think about things differently, or perhaps think about things you haven't thought about in a while. Whether you know it or not, you have a lot of things in your life running on autopilot. When you brush your teeth, for example, you don't give much thought to it. Your brain does what it needs to automatically and you probably think about at least a dozen other things while you brush. It's great that your brain can program these tasks in so you can be free to pay attention to things that are more important. Can you imagine if you had to give conscious thought to every move you made? Your brain has such a big job that automatic or unconscious thought patterns help you to be much more efficient. Your brain wants to put as many things on autopilot as it possibly can.

Obviously, brushing your teeth or washing your hair are useful automatic experiences. But there are a lot of automatic patterns in your brain that need to be interrupted if you're going to live your best life. The way you think about life will create your experience of life. I want to help *you create the experience that you want.*

As with all of the concepts in this book, it's not my job to tell you what you "should" do. You are the only one qualified to know what's best for you because it's your life. I'll teach you simple ways to shift away from the extra responsibilities that you no longer want. But it's not about telling you that you shouldn't do so much for your kids, because that's not really any of my business. I'll simply raise your awareness so that you can make decisions at a conscious level rather than by default.

We are starting with the Mom Autopilot trap because, well… it's really where all of the traps begin.

So, let's think back.

Do you remember when you brought your first child home from the hospital? No matter how long ago that was, you probably remember it well. Just a few days earlier, you had only been responsible for yourself, and now, there you were, responsible for all the needs of another (helpless) human being. Every wince, every cry, every movement was a clue that your child needed something. It was up to you to figure out what that was and take care of it.

Talk about a major learning curve.

For me personally, I thought I had a lot figured out before having kids. I was an achiever, a doer, a make-it-happen kind of girl. But when I had kids, it felt like the rug was pulled out from under me. Why didn't the secrets and tips work for my baby? How did such a little human create so much laundry? And how in the world was I really supposed to function on so little sleep?

Looking back, this is where it started. My brain, trying to manage the overload of new jobs and responsibilities, started to develop Mom Autopilot as a coping mechanism.

Initially, Mom Autopilot was a life-saver.

This phase of intense care-taking programmed and installed your brilliant Mom Autopilot, and thank goodness, right? It made you a super-ninja. It helped you survive sleep deprivation and still figure out all the new unknowns like colic and mystery fevers.

It was an extremely useful brain setting at that time, but it may not be anymore. At least not in the ways that so many moms continue to use it. You rely so heavily on autopilot that you jump into taking care of things even when you don't need to. You don't even think about it. You are so programmed to be aware (and take care of) everyone's needs that you just… do it.

Someone is sad? Let me fix that. Someone needs shoes? It's already on my list. You see what needs fixing, and you do it. Boom.

Why is this so important?

This small concept can improve your quality of life and offer you the relief that no schedule or planning system alone can offer—the kind of relief that comes when there's less pressure and more time, energy, and fun.

The kind of relief that every woman deserves.

HABITS THAT WEAR YOU OUT

As you read, take a minute to think about each habit and see if/how/ when you are falling into it. The questions in the workbook will help you get some clarity too so go ahead and download that now if you haven't yet. Some of your tendencies will be obvious, and the ideas here will be the key to major change! Others may offer just a little insight. Take what you need and leave the rest.

Habit 1: Not Questioning Your To-Do list (The Physical List)

This habit has to do with the tangible list in your planner or shoved in your purse, and yes, it's just like it sounds. You have a to-do list, and you don't question it often enough or critically enough. You're just proud you've got your list written, and you go full force until you get it done or run out of time.

But let's take a minute.

Who writes your to-do list each week? Really think about this.

Is it the school bulletin? The church newsletter? Your kids' never-ending demands?

Who determines what's important enough to make it onto your list?

My client Jennifer felt like no matter how hard she tried, she could never get it all done. She had a never-ending list that caught every task within a mile. Like so many of us, she usually thought there were "never enough hours in the day."

Worst of all, she felt guilty that she was too busy to spend quality time with her family. She was frustrated that she didn't exercise more, but who has the time? She was a slave to her schedule, not to mention constant feelings of guilt and obligation.

But Jennifer's problem wasn't that there was really "too much to do" or "not enough hours in the day." The problem was the way she was thinking and the pressure and worry it created for her. People-pleasing was running her life and wearing her out. And how did this show up? She didn't question her list. Her mindset was the problem; a jam-packed list was the symptom.

She didn't see that a lot of what she was doing was optional. She didn't know she could say "no" to things when everyone expected her to say "yes."

Like Jennifer, you may think you "have" to do what's on your list.

I've found that's never true. My clients will come to me with a list they are sure is merely the necessities, but after a few minutes, they start to see that there are more options than they ever realized.

So, how about you? Go ahead and think about a time when you've learned this about your list too...

Remember that day when you were completely overwhelmed with too much to do? You looked at your list, looked at the clock, and realized, "Something's got to give!"

What did you do? You found a way to simplify, delegate, and make the most important things happen.

You took the time to *question your list.*

Can you imagine what would be different if you could incorporate this practice of simplifying more often? How much more time would you have to spend on what's more important? How much more freedom would you feel when you knew you could get everything you really needed to do done?

Part of Jennifer's challenge was believing she couldn't say no. She told me, "It's hard for me to say no," and as a result, she always found a way to accommodate everyone at the expense of her own well-being. This is where we start to use the "the model" that I introduced in the Expectations chapter to see how it impacts our daily life. Here's what Jennifer's CTFAR model looked like:

Her **Circumstance** was: A full life with four kids.

Her **Thought** was: It's hard to say no.

Her **Feeling** was: Obligation.

The **Action** she took was: Putting everything asked of her on her to-do list.

Her **Result** was: Being exhausted from taking on too much.

When Jennifer thinks, "It's hard to say no," she feels obligated. The feeling of obligation drives her to do everything asked of her. When she takes this action, she spreads herself too thin, which results in exhaustion from doing too much.

Can you see that this result proves the thought, "It's hard to say no"? Since she believes that it's hard to say no, she doesn't. As a result, she is exhausted. This thought is creating a cycle of taking on too much without any option of saying no or questioning her list.

You may not think, "It's hard to say no," is just a thought, but it is. It's nothing more than something she thinks. Some people think, "It's easy to say no," and they have a completely different experience of life. The first step for Jennifer was helping her see that sentence for what it was—just a *thought* that was creating a negative experience for her.

Now, I could easily tell Jennifer that she "should" say no, but remember: Jennifer believes the thought, "It's hard to say no." If I believe something is hard and someone tells me to do it, I won't want to! Or I'll at least need a very compelling reason to try. The same goes for Jennifer. She either needed to have a different thought or belief about saying no or a compelling reason to do something hard.

We decided to do both.

I talked with Jennifer about what it was costing her when she didn't say no. It was costing her sleep, peace of mind, quality time with her kids, and a few other things that were really important to her. We spent a lot of time exploring this so that she could decide for herself if learning to say no would be worth it. For Jennifer, she could see that her life and her family members' lives would change drastically for the better if she was able to make "no" a more common response to the requests made of her.

Believe it or not, you can do this too. If you believe that it's hard to say no, go ahead and make a list of the ways saying yes all the time impacts your family. What is it costing you? Are you okay with this, or do you want more out of life? What would it mean for you if you created a new habit?

Next, Jennifer and I looked at the thought, "it's hard to say no." Believing this was not serving her. We talked about how a lot of people have no problem saying no, so it must not be true that it's hard to do. We also talked about things she has an easy time saying no to. For instance, if someone offered her illegal drugs, she would say no right away. We started to loosen the thought in her mind that it's hard to say no, and she began to see that this thought was optional. Saying no was only hard if she believed it was. We further talked about some ways she could reframe her thoughts about saying no. We came up with, "I'm learning to say no," "Saying no helps me say yes to what's most important," and, "I'm allowed to say no."

These thoughts rang true to her and were very empowering. They were new, but she believed them. They weren't automatic or go-to thoughts yet, but she started using them to change the way she was thinking, which led to different actions and results.

Circumstance: A full life with four kids.

Thought: Saying no helps me say yes to what's important.

Feeling: Curious and purposeful.

Action: Taking the time to evaluate what's most important and saying no when she chooses.

Result: More time and energy for what's most important.

As you can see, by changing the way she thought about saying no, she was able to feel and act differently. She was able to say no while feeling curious and purposeful rather than while feeling guilty. By saying no with positive intention, she was able to feel empowered. Sometimes, Jennifer still has a hard time saying no, but she has an understanding that it's only because of her thinking. She can remind herself that she gets to choose the way she thinks about her life and what that creates for her.

If you relate to Jennifer, you can borrow some of these thoughts or create your own. It's easy to Post-it note them on your schedule so you're reminded of them and your ability to shape your to-do list in a way that feels good to you.

> *"Learn to say 'no' to the good so you can say 'yes' to the best."*
> –John C. Maxwell

Habit 2: Running Mental Checklist (The Mental List)

This habit is all about the invisible list shoved into every corner of your brain. It runs all day and all night in your mind; let's face it, many of your to-dos are unwritten.

You may have an automatic habit of taking on all the requests and "needs" thrown at you from your kids. In the midst of family chaos, when your child calls out with something they need, it lands directly on this list written only in your mind.

Just like it did for Amy.

Amy is a go-getter. She is extremely organized and high-achieving and was always busy taking care of her family's needs. Her son would shout out from his room, "Mom, don't forget I need gym shorts." When her daughter would get in the car after school, she'll tell her all about her day, then throw into the conversation, "Oh, and I need a ride to school in the morning." No matter what was going on, her kids didn't hesitate to let her know what they needed whenever it came to them.

Amy, trying to keep up, was always in "get it done" mode (a.k.a. auto-pilot). She was so busy trying to stay afloat that she rarely questioned what was asked of her. She would immediately start figuring out *when and how she would squeeze it in.*

What about you? Is a running mental checklist cluttering up your mind around the clock like Amy? Is it weighing on you and leaving you feeling cranky, overwhelmed, and underappreciated as it swirls around in your brain?

Amy's mindset was one of one of "there's too much to do," which was driving her Mom Autopilot tendency. This thought caused her to feel anxious, driving her to take immediate action for every request thrown her way. Her result was a busy and rushed life day after day.

Circumstance: Mom of two; life.

Thought: There's too much to do.

Feeling: Anxious.

Action: Taking on every request without question and acting immediately.

Result: Always feeling busy and rushed.

You can see that her result proves the original thought, "There's too much to do." She was always on the go, never taking a moment to consider slowing down that running mental checklist, nor does she think to intercept that request before it becomes a "must-do." As we talk about solutions later in the chapter, you'll see that for Amy, and for you, it's a combination of a mind shift and brain training to create a simpler way of life.

Habit 3: Solving Every Problem (The Emotional List)

This habit is about the secret list of emotional to-dos that you never knew existed. It's the worry that sits in your stomach or weighs on your shoulders. This is the habit that most of my clients are completely unaware of, yet changing it is magic.

In one of my online coaching groups, Sara brought up a problem her son was having with another child teasing him. She explained the situation and asked me for advice. She wasn't sure of the best way to help him. She was hoping for the answer from me, but instead I asked, "Does he want your help?"

The call went silent. Every woman on the call was almost immediately confused. Someone even piped in, "Wait, what?"

Sara, of course, had no idea if he wanted her help or not: "I guess I just assumed that I need to help him with the problem. I mean, it's not okay that he's being teased, and I want to help him learn the best way to handle it."

You see, she was in the mindset and habit of *solving every problem*—always assuming it was her job to find solutions to the problems that presented themselves.

As we talked, we came to realize that her son was letting off steam when he brought it up with her. He was processing what was going on and thinking about solutions out loud. He didn't really want her to "solve" his problem; he just wanted a listening ear. The more Sara thought about it, she realized he had been handling the situation pretty well so far. She could also see that he was perfectly capable of figuring it out and standing up for himself.

She had been worried and ruminating on a problem that *wasn't actually hers to solve*. The thought, "I need to solve his problems," was so automatic that it left no room for curiosity. This thought was tied into what a "good mom" would do, so it was hard for her to see other options.

Start to notice how often you jump to solving problems, and you will likely be pretty surprised to realize that not every problem needs you. If you're highly empathic (like me), then trying to solve other people's emotions and problems comes naturally to you. When it comes to our kids, breaking this habit requires extreme awareness and a paradigm shift to understand how much better it will be (for everyone) if we can stop believing we need to solve every problem they face. As you do, this emotional list will begin to disappear.

So, how often are you *solving every problem*? Go ahead, think about how often this comes up for you. Use the workbook questions to uncover when this is most common for you and why. That personal insight will be extremely revealing.

Why Are You Stuck in These Exhausting Habits?

You can see that Mom Autopilot really is an extension of that first phase of motherhood that is defined by mega-responsibility for the well-being of a helpless human. It now shows up as more on your to-do list than necessary, taking on requests at any moment without interception, or simply believing you need to solve your kids' problems all the time.

These automatic responses leave you feeling as though you're at the mercy of your life rather than being in the driver's seat. This feeling is totally unnecessary. So why are you stuck in this automatic pattern?

- You are unaware.

Until now, you may not have realized that you were taking things on that you didn't need to. After all, it's called "autopilot" for a reason—it just kind of happens unless we consciously do something different.

- You don't understand the negative impact it's having.

Even if you knew you could take on less, you didn't realize the extra weight it is putting on your shoulders. Perhaps you didn't realize that it's causing you to feel stuck, unappreciated, or unhappy in your life and that it impacts your kids too.

- You don't know that it's optional.

Taking on these extra responsibilities and solving every single problem are totally optional. As you continue reading this book, you will learn that so much about *your thoughts and your experience of life is optional.* The way you think, feel, behave, and experience life is in your hands.

- You are a people pleaser.

Eliminating things from your list and saying no sometimes means others won't like it. You get to decide if you are willing to experience that discomfort if it means a better way of life for you and your family.

- You take on other people's emotions.

If you have empathic qualities, you may find it extremely difficult to shift away from solving problems when they come up. What I want to teach you is that as an empath, it's even more important for you to learn this skill. There is mounting evidence that highly sensitive people are prone to ailments like chronic fatigue syndrome, autoimmune disease, hormonal imbalances, and digestive problems. Learning how to recognize what problems are yours to solve and which are not is a vital skill to your long-term well-being.

NEW MINDSETS + NEW HABITS

… the liberating, energizing, superwoman kind that will rock your world.

You've already gotten some insight on how my clients did things differently. Now, I'm going to give you some concrete actions you can put into practice too. These aren't just empty habits, but they work alongside the mindset shifts you're working toward. Pick one or two, and give them a try. Leave the rest for another day.

Solution 1: Priorities

Before you can know what you want to clear from your list, your head, and your shoulders, it's helpful to decide what your priorities are. This mega-solution is the starting point to all things intentional so you can create the new habits you want in your life.

But a lot of us freeze when we think about listing priorities. What about you? Are you thinking right now, "Oh, that's a good idea. I'll have to do that later when I can set aside some time"?

It's easy to overcomplicate and think we need to schedule a time to soul-search, go on a retreat to make a vision board, and use a guided journal.

You don't need to do any of that.

You don't need to spend a lot of time, and you don't need to get it "right."

You can simply start where you are now.

All you need is a pencil with a good eraser.

Remember though, whatever your priorities are, they are not the same as mine. Think about what's most important to YOU, rather than me, your neighbor, or your friend. Creating new thought patterns and habits will take effort, so you want to make sure you're doing the work that's aligned with what you really want.

So, what are your priorities?

Write them down **now**. List five. (And don't worry, you can re-write them or adjust them anytime. That's why you're using a pencil.)

1.

2.

3.

4.

5.

That wasn't so bad, was it?

You've just identified the five things that are most important to you. This is a simple a tool to help raise your awareness of what you are creating in your life vs. what you want to create.

"The key is not to prioritize what's on your schedule, but to schedule your priorities." –Stephen R. Covey

As you look at your priority list, rearrange it if you need to so you can rank them in order of importance. This means that whatever is most important would be placed at number one. (It doesn't mean that number one takes the most time.) Sometimes we panic over listing our priorities in order because we somehow equate time with importance, but that's just not true. Whatever is in spot number one needs to get *enough time*, but not necessarily the most time.

Why do we rank them? Ranking your priorities helps you make decisions. It's an automatic (good automatic) decision-making tool. Remember, we want to use automatic responses to our advantage, not to our detriment. As you list and rank your priorities, you create a system you can rely on to help you make decisions about your list of responsibilities. It's no longer about whether or not you "should" do something. It's about making a decision that's aligned with your priorities.

Here's what I mean. Let's say there is a community function that you feel obligated to go to even though you haven't had family time in a while. If you've already decided that family time is a higher priority than community time, then the decision is simple. Make sense?

You can take these five priorities, write them on a 3x5 index card, and put them next to your bed, in your agenda, or on your fridge. Keep them somewhere you can refer to them when you're making your to-do list. This is a way of helping guide you as you begin to eliminate unnecessary responsibilities from your life. It's simple, fast, and most of all, *enlightening*.

With your priorities in front of you, you'll naturally spend more time on those and less on the things that aren't as important to you. You'll be *doing more by doing less*—more focus on priorities and less time wasted on things that aren't important.

Solution 2: Question Your List and Intercept Requests

This solution is not rocket science, but a simple matter of training your brain to create a practical habit that will give you back some precious time. It's a new automatic system to replace the old one that's giving you too much to do. This solution will help you both with the tangible to-do list and the mental checklist.

"Good habits are worth being fanatical about." –John Irving

Every morning for the next week, after you've written your to-do list, ask yourself the following questions:

1. What do I need to do?

2. What do I want to do?

3. What can someone else do?

4. Does this align with my priorities?

5. What can I take off the list right now?

This process might add two to three minutes to your morning, but imagine how much time it will free up! I know that eliminating things from your list will present challenges, specifically fear, resistance, and worry about letting things go. They are all normal, and I'm going to help you out with those in the workbook.

In order to apply this to the running mental checklist, we want to train your brain to create a pause and intercept those frequent requests and thoughts of "I need to" before they become a must on your list. Imagine if there was a pause button on that moment someone asked something of you and when you took on the request. Could it be that some of those requests wouldn't end up on your to-do list at all?

One trick I love to use is practicing the phrase, "I'll consider it." When a request is thrown at you or your brain starts assigning things to your mental checklist, practice saying, "I'll consider it," or, "I'll get back to you." This is the perfect way for you to address the request and remind yourself that it's optional whether or not you will take it on. It gives you permission to consider it at a later time when you are looking at your to-do list (and priorities). By considering the request at a specific time, you will be more intentional and clear about whether you are or are not going to do it.

You can also use the questions from the list above throughout the day. Post them on the dashboard of your car, on your phone, at your desk, or on your fridge. The more you can get in the habit of finding out what you really need to do and what you don't, the more you'll find your list becoming much more manageable and your mood much better!

A lot of my clients love using a request box for their kids. It's a simple box with paper that requests can be placed in, creating a "pause" between the request and when it ends up on mom's to-do list. So simple, but it's the perfect tool to get out of Mom Autopilot.

These simple habits of questioning your list and intercepting requests are extremely useful new patterns for you. It may seem clunky or awkward at first, but as you train your brain, it will become second nature to you. I remember my typing class in 9th grade when every keystroke was torture. It took so much brain power to remember what key to push without looking down at my hands on the keyboard, and it seemed that I would never learn to type.

Now as I write this book, I'm completely focused on the message I want to send you, and my hands cooperate effortlessly. My brain and body have been trained with a skill, and it's now automatic.

The same is true as you create new habits and thought patterns. If you practice, these will become automatic ways of thinking. Not only will the questions be effortless, but your list of to-dos will become shorter and more meaningful. You will create a life in which you do the things that matter most to you. You won't be overburdened, but instead spend your time in the ways you want to the most.

A few more things to think about when it comes to questioning your list:

Just because your kids want something doesn't mean they need it.

Just because your kids think they need something doesn't mean they do.

Just because *you* think your kids need something doesn't mean they do.

Just because you are invited doesn't mean you need to say yes.

Just because it's a "good cause" doesn't mean it needs to be your priority.

Just because you have an opportunity doesn't mean you need to take it.

Just because your child is sad doesn't mean you need to fix it.

As you start to take on only those things you really need/want to do, you'll free up your time and energy. You'll also automatically make room for the rest of your family to step up to their own responsibilities. You are doing more by doing less—encouraging and cultivating responsibility in your kids while taking more off of your plate.

Solution 3: Curiosity

The last solution already warmed up your sense of curiosity. Now, we'll get even more specific and see how curiosity clears up more than just the mental checklist; it's the key to eliminating that secret list of emotional needs so you can get out of the habit of solving everyone's problems.

Remember Sara and her son's problem that wasn't hers to solve? She was assuming he needed/wanted her help, and had the thought, "I need to solve his problems." Sara realized that her son's problem wasn't hers to solve; it was his. She also realized that *this was just one example of a pattern she had of constantly taking on his problems.*

Because of her belief that she needed to solve his problems, she left no room for curiosity. This once-useful pattern that kept her son fed and alive as a baby was not useful anymore.

Our coaching focused on raising her awareness and therefore shifting her beliefs about what she needed to take on. We took a look at her model and what it was creating.

Circumstance: Mom with a son who has (normal) problems.

Thought: I need to solve his problems.

Feeling: Panicked.

Action: Taking instant action to solve his problems without hesitation.

Result: She was always solving his problems.

This result was so familiar that she continued to believe it was her job to solve everything, thus reinforcing the initial thought, "I need to solve his problems."

The key to changing this pattern for Sara was curiosity.

> *"Curiosity is the wick in the candle of learning."*
> –William Arthur Ward

If you are in the habit of solving every problem, think about how you can begin to approach problems like a detective—with curiosity and by asking a lot of questions.

You can use questions to help you feel curious and interrupt the automatic pattern of solving problems. This is a way for you to create new patterns of thought with new actions.

For the first little while, you may want to keep this information handy so you can remember to do it.

When your kids come to you and lay a problem at your feet, first take the time to listen (just listen!)

If you notice the "solve every problem" mentality taking over, go ahead and:

- Stop and ask yourself if your child needs your help.
- Ask your child if they want your help.
- Ask yourself: Do you want to help them, or do you want them to figure it out on their own?

Ask, ask, ask.

Only you have the answer to how much or how little you want to get involved.

By allowing them to share, think about, and solve their own problems, you are making them less dependent on you, while turning them into *awesome* problem solvers.

You'll be encouraging them to ask you for help when they need it, rather than assuming that you'll take care of everything automatically.

An added bonus is that your kids will feel like they can talk to you and you will listen without trying to take control of the situation.

It's another example of doing more by doing less.

You can take this further in the workbook and discover how this plays out for you.

THE RECAP

As you can see, there is a very good reason you feel so much pressure, stress, and so overwhelmed. Your desire to give your best created patterns that aren't useful. The automatic setting in your brain, Mom Autopilot, is putting more on your list of things to do than necessary, and it's also creating unnecessary worry about your kids and how you're doing as a mom.

You are over-responsible, and you feel it taking a toll.

You need to have that weight lifted off of your shoulders, and now you know how.

You can start by:

- Raising your awareness of the habits and traps you're falling into, including:

    ◦ Not questioning your physical list

    ◦ Keeping a running mental checklist

- ○ Solving every problem; creating an emotional list that wears you out

- Implementing the solutions listed here:

  - ○ Create five ranked priorities. Give yourself two minutes (maximum) to do it.

  - ○ Use the questions provided to evaluate your list every day. This should add about three minutes to the start of your day.

  - ○ Practice the phrase, "I'll consider it," when you have requests or new to-dos thrown your way. This will create a pattern of interrupting new requests before they end up on your running mental checklist. Use a request box to help train your kids as well.

  - ○ Get curious when your kids have a problem. Ask the questions provided to consider if they need/want/should have your help.

- Pay attention to what comes up for you as you work on this. Use the workbook to evaluate your thoughts so you can better understand how to make positive changes.

The Benefits

There are so many benefits to turning off Mom Autopilot.

You'll clear your life of things that don't matter and fill it with exactly what you want. You'll have less stress and pressure because you'll be focusing only on your responsibilities and not everyone else's. You will feel more in control of your own time and experience of life. You'll improve your relationships because as you clear away the extra obligation and worry, you'll become more emotionally available. You'll cultivate responsibility and problem-solving skills in your kids—skills they will need to be successful as adults.

As you do less physically and emotionally, you'll open the door to do more of what's most important and most joyful, starting down the path to finding your own version of happiness as a mom.

To access the workbook, visit:

www.mollyclaire.com/HappyMomMindsetWorkbook

Trap 2

Always on Call: 24/7 Expectations

THE TRUTH:
You are meant to grow, become, and succeed, and you have been given all the time you need to do that. You can trust the process of life and trust that time is on your side. It's never true that too much is expected of you. You're capable of doing your life in the time you've been given.

"The bad news is time flies. The good news is you're the pilot."
–Michael Altshuler

THE TRAP: MOM IS ALWAYS ON CALL

My friend Julie is a nurse, and she rarely makes plans when it's her weekend to be on call. She doesn't know if she will get called in or not, but she has learned that if she makes plans, she will get the call.

She feels like it's not worth the trouble to make plans, get excited for them, and then have to cancel at the last minute. It's much easier for her to just block out that time and be ready to go in to the hospital.

Usually, this means that she doesn't get as much accomplished or misses out on getting together with friends.

This works out okay for her—after all, she is only on call once in awhile.

If she were on call 24 hours a day, can you imagine how it would impact her life? She wouldn't be very productive. She would likely miss out on a lot of social opportunities. She would probably feel like a slave to her schedule. Most likely, she would feel very little control over her own life, and that's a pretty discouraging place to be.

As moms, it's easy for us to fall into the trap of believing we are always on call 24/7, especially when there have been plenty middle-of-the-night disruptions and emergencies.

We get so used to accommodating the last minute needs that come up that we've created a mindset of believing we are always on call. Of course, there's some degree of truth to it. If our kids need something, we want to be there for them. However, I want to show you how this pattern of thinking may be making your life harder than it needs to be.

The truth is, sometimes we take it a little too far.

It's easy for us to get so used to being on call and allowing guilt to make our decisions that we give up all rights to having schedules of our own. It's hard for us to say no to a last minute request from our kids and not feel bad about it. It's a challenge to have clear boundaries for when we are available to our oh-so-needy kids and when we are not. When we *think* we are always on call, we *feel* stressed or overwhelmed, and *behave* as if we are always on call. This leaves us little room for freedom in our lives or our schedules, but it doesn't have to be this way.

Kids are needy. And the more we give, the more they "need."

Kids take cues from us to understand what they should ask of us.

What cues are we giving them? Let's explore this a bit and find out how you can free yourself from the "always on call" trap. Freedom awaits you, mama!

Let's start with a few questions:

- When your kids call for you, do you feel the need to drop everything and respond?
- Do you find yourself calling out in an annoyed voice, "Just a minute!!!"?
- Do you have a hard time setting limits on when you are available to help with homework or a ride to a friend's house?
- Does it frustrate you when your child expects something of you *right now*?
- Do you feel like your kid's schedule is a priority over yours, rather than it finding its place within yours?
- When your child has a major project that they put off until the last minute, do you change your plans to help them get it finished?

If you answered yes to any of these, you're falling into the "always on call" trap in one way or another.

Falling into this trap can cause you to feel irritable and worn out. You're likely frustrated that you don't have more freedom in your life. You wish your family respected your time more and would stop taking you for granted. By recognizing the "on call" thought patterns and beliefs, you can reclaim your schedule. You can feel good about the time you give to your kids and great about the time you don't. By changing the way you think about your time, you'll change the way you experience time.

Why do I want to teach you this?

I want to teach you this because of Molly. Yes, that's me.

When I began my coaching work, I could clearly see that I struggled with this trap. I had a really hard time setting boundaries around what time was my own and what time I was available to my family. My kids would bring me things to take care of late at night at the last minute. I felt constant pressure because I thought I could never have downtime. The only time they would leave me alone was when I had a migraine—not a very pleasant way to spend my only time free from their demands.

I quickly realized as I coached more and more women that this was a trap that most of us get stuck in.

As I changed my way of thinking and moved toward setting limits on my availability, I was able to create time to do what I wanted to do. I was able to achieve more success in my business, take better care of myself, and use my downtime in more enjoyable ways (and I get migraines much less often). When I remember that I'm in charge of my time, I feel so much more freedom and less pressure. I'm more productive, more present, and much more engaged with everyone. The shift in my mindset creates an increase in my happiness.

Remembering that I am in charge of my time is a conscious practice for me. This book and these solutions are about creating practices and continuing to practice them. It's not about immediate change or flipping a switch. It's most definitely not about perfection. It's about awareness, desire to change, and practice.

THE PERSONALITIES: WHICH "ON CALL" MOM ARE YOU?

Let's take some time to identify exactly how you fall into this trap. Depending on your personality, beliefs, and thought patterns, this trap will show up in different ways for you. I'm going to give an overview and specifics on each one. As you read through, you'll be able to recognize which category you fall into.

Remember, this isn't a judgement, but rather an awareness of thought patterns and behaviors that may or may not be serving you. As you identify with one of these personalities, you can evaluate if this pattern is working for you or not. Is it helpful or stressful? Is it giving you more freedom and peace or causing you to feel stuck?

Dr. Mom

Imagine standing in a hospital hallway. Echoing through the hall is the sound of the intercom: "Paging Dr. Mom."

When Dr. Mom is given a request, she drops everything, always accommodating requests with little regard for what she had previously planned. Dr. Mom responds immediately, no matter what. She believes it is her duty as a mom to be there the moment help is needed. If you fit into this category, you probably don't really see it as a problem. You want to accommodate and work around your kids' schedules because you see that as part of your job description.

And it may not be a problem if it's working for you…

But is it?

The biggest issue my Dr. Mom clients have is that they find it hard to have their own sense of identity, separate from being "mom." Giving their time constantly doesn't feel like a problem, but they miss their own sense of self. Many of them also see that giving up the role of Dr. Mom has benefits for their kids. Something to think about…

Annoyed Mom

Annoyed Mom is not going to be taken advantage of. She will lay down the law and let her kids know that she has a life too. When the kids demand her time or expect her to work around their schedules, she is annoyed!

She can't believe they are so demanding.

If you are Annoyed Mom, you may say things like, "You know, I can't drop everything for you all the time!" or perhaps, "Don't you know I have things to do to?!"

You might *think* you are standing up for yourself, but you're not. You might *think* that you're not "on call" when you say those things, but actually… you are.

Let's take a look at those thoughts.

Think of a recent request that led to an Annoyed Mom response. Why did you feel annoyed by it?

You probably had thoughts lurking in the background like, "I should do this for them," or "I want to be a good mom." Or perhaps, "I shouldn't put myself first."

These are the thoughts that keep my Annoyed Mom clients in this trap.

Karen was really frustrated about how demanding her kids were, but the major belief that kept her stuck was the idea that if someone expects something of her, she's *supposed* to do it. When her kids or her husband would make a request, she didn't feel she was allowed to say, "I'm not available right now." (By the way, she didn't even realize this was happening!)

For her, it was an instinctual reaction when they asked something of her. During our calls, we spent a lot of time looking at this belief and how it was affecting so much of her life. Her frustration with those around her was all about her own belief that she wasn't allowed to say no and protect her own needs and wants. Doing this work allowed her to take better care of herself and create some joy and success in her life, leaving the guilt behind.

Frazzled Mom

Frazzled Mom is always putting out fires. It's hard for her to set her own schedule because no matter what, there always seems to be an emergency. If you are Frazzled Mom, you feel like you have little control over your schedule. You're not sure how you can ever accomplish things *you* want because something always pops up. Life feels like a game of Whack-A-Mole. You are always responding to things that are urgent and playing catch up. It's impossible to plan because you're always behind.

What do I mean by things that are "urgent"?

In Stephen R. Covey's book, *The 7 Habits of Highly Effective People*, he talks about the difference between urgency and importance.

Things that are urgent demand your immediate attention. The doorbell rings, the cell phone buzzes, or a notification pops up on your desktop. These things create a sense of urgency and can take your attention away from something important in order to deal with them right away.

Things that are important are the things that actually matter; for example, quality time with our kids. We all believe it's most important to focus there, right? Yet when I'm reading with my daughter and my phone starts buzzing, it creates a (false) sense of urgency. It's a competition between what's urgent and what's important.

So what about you? If you are having a conversation with someone and your phone rings, do you feel the need to respond to the urgency of the call? Or do you focus on the relationship and conversation that is important, even though it's not pressing?

This is a good time to reflect on how you respond to urgent vs. important matters in all areas of your life and you can use the workbook to do that. This is obviously much more than a "mom" problem. It's pretty much a worldwide epidemic.

If you respond to urgency, chances are you are falling into the "always on call" trap with your kids (and you're probably pretty frazzled a lot of the time). By now, your brain might be thinking about all the ways you are always putting out fires. You may even be wondering if it is possible to have a life where you're *not* always putting out fires. Yes, it is. Let's talk about it.

Mom Personalities: The Recap and Why

Whatever personality type you identify with, you are allowing everyone and everything else to dictate your schedule. Is it any wonder that we can feel so "stuck" as moms when it comes to our time? It makes sense that we always feel behind, overwhelmed, and often underappreciated when we give everyone else the power to make demands for us and our time.

So, why do we do it? Well, because we are givers and caretakers. It's because we feel a responsibility to our families and we've forgotten that first and foremost, we have a responsibility to ourselves. You can see how closely related this is to Mom Autopilot, because we simply don't think about it. We are in the habit of basing our schedule off of everyone else's needs and forgetting that we are a person with needs and wants too.

Just like Mom Autopilot, it's a brain trap. It's a way of thinking that has us stuck and powerless. The upside is that if this trap starts in our brains, it can end in our brains. The solution to a new approach to your time, how you use it, protect it, and view it is changing the way you think about it. To get started, take some time to think through or journal these questions. You can also continue this in the workbook with more detail.

1. Is always being available benefitting your kids? Why or why not?

2. Is it what you want to do? Why or why not?

3. Would you see any benefit to creating your schedule first and building their schedule into yours? How would that feel?

4. Would there be any advantages for your child if they knew they needed to ask ahead of time or find a different solution? Would it benefit them to understand that you have needs too?

SIMPLE TRICKS FOR NEW THOUGHT PATTERNS

Solution 1: Create an Intentional Life (Dare I Say It? Time Management)

What exactly is an intentional life? It is one that you choose. It is on purpose. It is doing the things you want and plan to do. To be intentional with your life, you need to be intentional with your thoughts, which also means being intentional with your time. Remember, YOU are in charge of your time.

"Either you run the day, or the day runs you." –Jim Rohn

But hearing "time management" can make you groan, especially if you feel like a big fat failure at it. I was never really that great at managing my time before I had kids, but I could still accomplish what

I needed to do. When I added kids and their accompanying chaos to the mix, time management seemed laughable.

A lot of my clients feel the same way, especially my "Mompreneur" clients. It seems impossible to run a viable business while holding down the home front. Time management sounds like a good idea until someone is sick or you're dealing with a rodent infestation or a broken A/C. (I may or may not be speaking from experience.)

The only way to change your ability to make and keep a schedule is to *change the way you think about it* when things don't go as expected. Making and keeping a schedule doesn't mean that everything will go as planned. It means you schedule, commit, and make it work—one way or another.

Time management in the life of a mom is much like Elizabeth Edward's quote:

"She stood in the storm and when the wind did not blow her way, she adjusted her sails."

Sometimes, we get stuck thinking about time management as black or white—either we stick to a schedule or we don't. This way of thinking just doesn't work when you're a mom because there has to be some wiggle room for important things that come up. I promise that it is possible to set a specific schedule, commit to it, and also be resourceful and creative to adapt as needed. It's an art, but you can learn… if you're willing to practice.

I had a great session with Becky in which we got extremely clear about her time. After years of being a full-time mom, she was adjusting to starting an at-home business. At the beginning of the session, we talked about how she had "so much to do" in order to get things going. She told me she "didn't know how to get it all done," and even admitted to me, "I don't know how you do it."

Becky had a lot of thoughts causing her to feel really frustrated, but I didn't believe that she had "so much to do," because that thought didn't really make sense. It was a vague thought, and it was confusing her. What was "so much"? What did that mean? Vague thoughts like this are the very things that keep us stuck and feeling overwhelmed.

The first thing we did was take that thought and get factual about it. Exactly how much do you have to do? We went through everything on her list, right down to the specifics. After we had each specific task defined, we assigned a time frame for each item.

You see, we were moving from the vague, overwhelming statement of, "I have so much to do," to the truth about what she actually needed to do to get her business going.

Once we had defined specific tasks and specific time frames, all that was left to do was to schedule them in. Within one hour, she went from feeling that her business would take a few overwhelming months to realizing she could have everything done and ready within two weeks!

Keep in mind this was taking into account all the daily tasks of life and kids, without carving out any extra time than she normally did. We got extremely clear about her work hours and set them in stone. We did this by finding out exactly what worked for her life, her kids, and her schedule. We didn't base it off of anyone else's business plan or expectation. We even built in some time to finish things up that may have taken longer than anticipated.

Getting mathematical about her time was an instant stress-reducer. She was much more mentally and emotionally available in her off time because she didn't have the weight of "so much to do" spinning in the back of her mind.

You'll find more specific guidance on this process in the workbook. This is one of my best tools, so make sure you access it and understand how you can apply it in your own life.

"There is no one busy in this world, it's always about priorities. You will always find time for the things you feel are important."
–Nishan Panwar

Another client of mine had a similar, yet totally different scenario. Melanie wanted help getting clear on her time and how to find balance being "Mom" and a business owner. She felt guilty that she didn't do more with her business. In our conversations, it sounded like she didn't work much on her business at all, but when we did the same exercise with her schedule, we found that she was working way more hours than she wanted to! She had so many things scheduled at varying times that she was spread too thin. Melanie was expecting herself to do 30 hours of tasks in a 24-hour period. While this may seem like bad news, it was actually great news for her! No wonder she felt like she didn't have enough time—she didn't! It's impossible to turn 24 hours into 30 hours. This was such valuable information for her because she knew without a doubt that she needed to cut things from her schedule. She could see that there was no way she could create what she wanted in her life if she was working with an unrealistic schedule. This is a great example of the need to get really factual and mathematical about time, because our perception of our time rarely reflects reality.

With this clarity, she was able to choose what she would keep and what she wouldn't. She felt immense relief when she created a schedule that was actually possible to accomplish. She felt empowered to think that she could dedicate the time she wanted to her family. She was excited with the idea of setting limits on the time her business was taking up. What had been vague before had now become clear. With awareness and clarity, we can choose what we want and make it happen.

As you can see, time management + mom life is possible. It's a practice that requires trial and error. When you plan to set your schedule, you can borrow some thoughts like, "I'm going to experiment with this," or, "I'll take a stab at this and see what I learn." Maybe, "This is a starting point."

These are reasonable "bridging" thoughts for you. You're not telling yourself, "This will be amazing," but rather giving yourself a thought that allows you to move forward with curiosity and a bit of hope.

Time management isn't a fun topic, but it's exciting when you think about creating an intentional life. When you see the possibilities for your life, your family, or your business, time management is a little more enticing. I love the freedom that it gives me and the weight it takes off my shoulders. Managing your time is a great way to see that **there's always plenty of time**. And if there's not, then something on your schedule isn't necessary.

Solution 2: Notice Urgent vs. Important

In the last chapter, we talked about priorities and how they tie directly into the "urgent vs. important" idea.

As I mentioned, this is a concept taught by Stephen R. Covey, and it's so simple and true to life. Being aware of the difference between urgency and importance is really the key to a conscious decision to change.

Responding to urgency is a habit. To change a habit, you must first require a desire to get a different result.

If you want to stop the cycle of playing Whack-A-Mole, or if you want to feel like you are in the driver's seat of your life, it's worth considering how you respond to urgency. You may notice a correlation between this habit and autopilot. Sometimes, our kids needs seem urgent to us even though they aren't important. Just as you need to make a conscious effort to shut off Mom Autopilot, you need to make a conscious effort if you want to stop responding to urgency.

"Where are you being reckless with your time?"
–The Life Coach School

A few questions for you:

- What would be different for you if you could focus on what's actually important?

- If you broke the cycle of responding to urgency, how would you benefit?

- Do you think it would be worth it to work toward a life where you get to focus on what is important rather than on what is urgent?

I've got some exercises in the workbook that will help you sort out the urgent vs. the important and get you started on changing this habit.

It's also important to talk about the thinking behind the response to urgency. Remember, every action you take is driven by a feeling, which begins with a thought. The way you are thinking about time creates your experience of time. Let's borrow from Becky in the example above, who believed she had "so much to do."

This is a common thought for women, and yet it wreaks havoc on our daily experiences. If I have a mindset that I have "so much to do," I'm usually feeling completely stressed out. I'm wound so tightly that I don't take a moment to consider if I'll respond to urgency or not. Let's take a look at what this way of thinking creates for us.

Circumstance: Phone buzzes while reading with daughter.

Thought: I have so much to do.

Feeling: Anxious.

Action: Responding to what's urgent.

Result: Thinking, "I have so much to do." I'm not intentional with my time. I end up giving away precious time to urgent things that don't really matter.

You can see that the result is giving up something that was important, which proves the thought, "I have so much to do." I'm left feeling spread thin and frustrated that I'm not keeping my own priorities. We'll explore a few more thought models toward the end of the chapter to see how your thoughts about time are impacting you.

Urgency comes from our thinking, and it's also an automatic habit. For me personally, when I choose to say no to urgency, I'm much calmer and can focus on what's important. I can think more clearly, and I have more energy. When I remember that ***there's always plenty of time***, it helps me stay focused on what's important vs. what's urgent.

"Ask yourself if what you are doing today is getting you closer to where you want to be tomorrow." –Anonymous

Solution 3: Protect Your Time

One extremely useful skill you can learn is how to protect your time. If you've scheduled time to work on a project or do something for yourself, what steps do you take to protect that time? This skill requires us to examine your thinking and how it's playing out for you.

Laura is a great example of how protecting our time is key to getting out of the "always on call" trap. She had set time aside to be a part of my online coaching program as part of her commitment to personal development. It was important to her, and she had carefully blocked off the time she needed to be there. Then, the very day we were talking about time management in the group, she received a call from her teenage daughter asking to be picked up early from school. We all laughed together at the irony of it all. We all knew how Laura felt, and the timing couldn't have been better. She was torn between staying on the call or heading to school.

We talked as she made her decision about what to do. She knew that her daughter would be fine for an extra 20 minutes. She wasn't in danger or in dire need. Laura wanted to keep her commitment to herself and protect her time even though she felt a little torn. This was the perfect opportunity for her to start resetting her brain regarding how she thinks about her time and what's required of her. This was the first tiny step in helping her believe that she could protect her time. She began to show herself that it was okay to have things that were important to her and free herself from the "always on call" trap. One tiny step goes a long way in leading a happier, more intentional life.

"You cannot expect your kids to respect your time if you don't respect your time." –Molly Claire

Just like Laura, it may be that protecting your time isn't easy for you, especially when you've scheduled time for yourself to relax or do your own thing. I learned the hard way how important it is for me to protect my personal time. As an achiever and a caretaker, creating "me" time didn't come naturally, but when I was hit with chronic fatigue syndrome, everything changed. I had to rest and nurture myself in a lot of ways just so I could be slightly available for my family. It was like torture for me. I was used to doing it all and going full speed, and there I found myself, barely able to get my kids out the door to school. As I moved through my recovery, I learned that achievers and caretakers often get CFS. It was only as I learned about the physical, mental, and emotional aspects of CFS that I learned how important it was to protect my time.

Now, nearly at full speed again, I have some rules that I've put in place for my kids (and me) to protect my time and well-being.

I require adequate sleep. Not excessive sleep (when I'm healthy), but adequate. I'm an early-to-bed kind of girl. As my kids were getting older, getting to bed early became more difficult. I was getting last minute requests for lunch money, getting a field trip slip signed, or a million and one other things that led me to realize that I needed to protect that part of my day. I set a rule that I'm closed after 9 p.m. Before 9:00, I'm generally pretty happy and helpful. If anyone comes to me after 9:00, there are no guarantees. I joke that I won't be held accountable for anything I say or do after 9 p.m. I'm closed. If you break into a store when it's closed… it's going to get messy.

Protecting my time meant I could take care of myself so that I could be a million times better for my family. I want to be happy, engaged, and completely available emotionally to my kids. I can only do that if I protect my time.

Making a plan to protect your time is pretty easy. Following through… that's when it gets tricky.

When my kids need something last minute, I have to be okay with letting them drop the ball. Sometimes, I may decide that I *will* accommodate what they bring me, but as a result, they are required to do extra chores the next day (which may be like pulling teeth). Protecting my time means that I may feel bad or risk them being unhappy, but I'm willing to do it. The benefits are too important to me, and that's what I focus on when I'm having a hard time sticking to my plan.

If you find yourself feeling bad or guilty about protecting your time, let me offer you this.

What if protecting your time is a gift to your kids? What if it's one of the best things you can do as a mom? When you are able to protect your time, your space, and your emotional well-being, you may find you'll be more relaxed, more energetic, more intentional, and happier. Isn't that the kind of woman you want to be and exactly what you hope to offer them?

Protecting your time is great for your kids too because it teaches them to plan ahead and take initiative and responsibility. It teaches them to respect your time and in turn, respect the time of others. So you can take great care of yourself, and give them an amazing gift—who knew?!

One of the best things it does for your kids? It models for them how to protect their own time and set their own limits. It gives them permission to protect themselves from excessive pressure in the future and practice healthy self-care habits early.

So as you step into this new space of protecting your time, here are a few key phrases you can use:

- I'm not available right now, but I can help you in an hour.

- The time I had available to sign permission slips has passed, but I can do it tomorrow.

- I'm sorry you forgot about your project, but I can't help you tonight.

- I want you to be able to go to your friend's house, but I need a day's notice if you need a ride.

Go ahead and create your own. Right now, think about when it's hard for you to protect your time. What might your response be? Thinking ahead and practicing is a great way to create new, permanent patterns.

I also love using a "do not disturb" sign on my door when I'm unavailable. There's something about having it in writing that reminds them (and me) that I'm off limits.

When I believe that **there's always plenty of time**, it helps me remember to make my own time a priority. It also helps reduce the sense of urgency to accommodate last minute requests and focus on what's important.

WHAT DO YOU MEAN THERE'S PLENTY OF TIME?

I started the chapter off telling you that there's plenty of time, and I keep talking about it. If you're still wondering what I'm talking about, I want to tell you about Angela.

Angela is a single mom who feels overwhelmed by the homework, dinner, and bedtime rush. She tries to make dinner and clean up, help her son who is struggling with math, and give loving attention at bedtime. One day, she came to our session feeling pretty overwhelmed and told me it feels like "there's never enough time."

Just like Becky, she had a thought about time that was causing her a lot of frustration and leading her to feel overwhelmed, so we decided to take a look at this thought to see what it was creating for her:

Circumstance: 24-hour days.

Thought: There's never enough time.

Feeling: Overwhelmed.

Action: Approaching homework help with little patience and ineffective use of her time.

Result: Math homework was made more difficult and took longer than expected. She ran out of time to do the other things she needed to do, which reinforced the thought, "There's never enough time."

When Angela believed there was never enough time, she felt so overwhelmed that she was frazzled and ineffective. She wasn't patient with her son, and as a result, they had arguments and power struggles. This, of course, made the task take longer than it otherwise would have. Her extreme level of stress was also wearing her out. This meant she was so tired that she crashed in bed before she could finish getting things in order. This was just another way that her actions reinforced the thought, "There's never enough time."

Angela and I were able to talk through what she believed about time and life. We discovered that she believed that God would never give her too much to do. She believed that she had the resources and gifts she needed to take care of her responsibilities. She also told me that she believed God wanted her to succeed and would therefore make it possible. All of these beliefs were in direct opposition to the idea that there was never enough time. She could see so clearly that what she really believed was that there was plenty of time to do what was important.

So, we tried it on for size, and I asked her an important question: *What if it's true that there's plenty of time to do what's most important?*

Immediately, she felt light and hopeful. She could now see clearly what things were important and what things could be let go. She could see how to spend her time differently to accomplish what she wanted to do. She also felt much more relaxed about the idea of helping her son. After all, if there was plenty of time to do it, she could be present and helpful rather than stressed about getting it over with.

Here's what happened:

Circumstance: 24-hour days.

Thought: There's plenty of time to do what's important.

Feeling: Hopeful.

Action: Focusing on the important things; being present and helpful with her son.

Result: She accomplished everything she needed to do, and didn't pass out from exhaustion, which reinforced the idea that there's plenty of time to do what's important.

This mindset shift was *the* difference for Angela. She could see that before, her brain had been clinging to a thought that wasn't true, and it was causing her a lot of problems.

As you can see, believing there's plenty of time isn't just thinking positively—it's setting yourself up to make it a reality. Your brain is so powerful that if you believe there is plenty of time, your brain will accommodate that belief and make it happen. It will awaken your subconscious to make that true. It's a powerful belief that can change everything when it comes to your time. It's empowering, hopeful, and will give you so much motivation to create that intentional life you are reaching for.

THE RECAP

We've talked a lot about beliefs around time, like, "There's so much to do," "There's never enough time," "Keeping a schedule is impossible," and, "I'm not allowed to set limits on my time."

All of these thoughts are creating negative feelings and negative results for you. As you change the way you think about time, the way you use your time will change as well. This will create an entirely different result for you, and suddenly, you'll be creating exactly what you want in your life!

You can start by:

- Raising your awareness. Notice how you think about time and read the stories in this chapter as a refresher. You are the one who gets to choose how you spend your time, so you might as well do it with intention rather than by default.

- Implementing the solutions listed here:

  ○ Clear up vague statements like, "There's so much to do" by getting mathematical. Be intentional with your time. Expect progress, not perfection.

- ○ Notice when you react to what's urgent. Decide what's important.

- ○ Protect your time no matter what! Create a "do not disturb" sign to remind your kids (and you) when you're not available. If you block time for something important to you, it's okay to ask som one else to wait... you *do* have a say in what you do with your time.

- Playing around with the idea that there's "plenty of time" or other thoughts you find useful. Think about what result you want to create and what beliefs will support that result. You can use the workbook to help you in this process.

Remember, the way you think about time will create your experience of time.

The Benefits

The best part about reclaiming your time? There are oh-so-many benefits!

As you begin to take ownership of your time, you'll feel empowered to create what you want in your life with less stress and burden weighing you down. Making a decision to respect your time will teach your kids to respect it as well. You'll teach them to be intentional, plan ahead, be less demanding, and be more responsible.

Freeing yourself from the "always on call" trap will allow you to stick to your priorities and stay true to your desires in life. It will give you the time you need to create a life of fulfillment and joy.

To access the workbook, visit:

www.mollyclaire.com/HappyMomMindsetWorkbook

Trap 3

Mom Comparison: Do It All and Fear of Missing Out

THE TRUTH:

Your soul is of great worth and so is the person sitting next to you. Infinite worth. Someone else's strength doesn't take away from yours. And your gifts don't put you above anyone else. There is room for each and every one of us to be great in our own capacity. Believe that you are capable of the life you've been given. You're the one who is qualified. Believe you can.

"No one is you and that is your power." –Dave Grohl

THE TRAP: MOM COMPARISON

As I start this chapter, I'm inclined to say that others have already said this better than I can. I want to say, "Go read what Brené Brown says about the finale of *Flashdance* and the myth of perfectionism."

And even as I say that, I'm falling into the very trap I'm talking about. I'm comparing.

It's easy to see what someone else has done and think that what you have to offer isn't worth much.

It's easy to think, "Why should I bother?" or to feel intimidated or inadequate.

While it's true that Brené Brown is incredible (and I do recommend her work), it's also true that my book is the one in your hands right now. I'm the vessel for this message in this moment. I have an opportunity to make a difference. And if I don't take this opportunity because I'm too worried that someone else could do it better... then I'll be right. Someone else will do it better because I won't be doing it at all. I'd miss out, you would miss out, and your kids would miss out on a mom who has learned how to appreciate her strengths and see her own worth.

As women, we already compare ourselves to others. When we become moms, the stakes automatically rise. We're embarking on something that we have no idea how to do, and there is such an impossible standard for what's expected.

Impossible standard + internal pressure to succeed + children who are individuals + no owner's manual = fear + doubt + worry.

When this fear, doubt, and worry creep in, the tendency to compare is multiplied, and you get stuck in the trap of "Mom Comparison." The worst part about this trap is that it only intensifies the doubt that we are already feeling. We doubt ourselves and our abilities, sometimes even mistakenly thinking that someone else could be a better mom than we can for our own child. As you may have guessed... this line of thinking won't create a very good result for you. Not to mention it feels pretty miserable.

You are capable of more than you realize.

Let's say my neighbor is a fantastic teacher who knows a lot about helping kids with ADHD. That doesn't mean that she would be a better mom for my ADHD son. It definitely doesn't mean that I'm deficient or doomed to fail.

I don't need to use her strength as a reason to feel bad about myself or doubt the role I play in my son's life. That line of thinking follows the assumption that we should all be the same. It evaluates everything around us as either better or worse, never taking individuality into account. It also completely ignores the fact that I am the one who was given *my* son in this life. It doesn't matter what she is amazing at; I'm the one who was chosen, which means I'm fully qualified. It means I'm the best possible person to do this job. Remembering this is extremely powerful for me.

And yes, *you* are the one who has been given *your* child. You're the one who is the most qualified to raise him. This is not by chance or accident, but exactly how it's supposed to be. Since you're supposed to be his mom, then of course you are 100% able to succeed in that endeavor. It wasn't a mistake, so of course you're qualified. Absolutely. *You're the one.*

You being "the one" doesn't mean that you don't reach out for help and rely on other's gifts. After all, that's why we're all here together in life, existing with different gifts and talents. It simply means that I never have to doubt if I'm good enough or capable of guiding, teaching, and raising him. *I don't need to doubt it because I know I'm meant to be his mom.* My belief is too strong and too powerful to be thrown off course by doubt.

Why does this matter so much?

If you compare yourself to all the best parts of everyone around you, you will fall short every time.

And believing that you are falling short day in and day out will paralyze you.

Understanding this is important because your kids deserve a mom who appreciates her own strengths and feels powerful and amazing. And you deserve to feel that way.

You've got way too much to offer and way too much to become

to live in the land of, "I'm not good enough." Besides, let's look at what this thinking will create for you...

Circumstance: Mom with a neighbor who is an ADHD expert.

Thought: I don't know what I'm doing; she is so much better than I am.

Feeling: Inadequate.

Action: Ruminating on thoughts of self-doubt and worry; thinking about all the ways you believe you are falling short.

Result: No positive result. You've closed yourself off from insight and wisdom because you believe you don't know what you're doing. You've created even more fear about your child and his fate.

As you look at this result, you can see that it will prove the original thought of, "You don't know what you're doing" and that someone else would be a better parent for your kid. Your mind will be so full of worry and doubt at this point that the original thought surely must be true.

This model is so common—you can probably change a few details and apply it to a million and one areas in your life. We're going to revisit this model later on in the chapter, but for now, remember: this line of thinking is optional. It's a habit, a pattern. The only reason it's easy for you to think this way is because you are used to it. As you shift your thought patterns, you create a different experience and a different result. You can escape the Mom Comparison trap with a little bit of effort and a mind shift.

COMPARE AND DESPAIR

Every time I read the concept of "compare and despair," it rings true. As women, we often feel inadequate because we are comparing ourselves to the woman next door, or more accurately, the picture we paint of the woman next door. We have such an idealistic picture of what our lives should be, and if we can't find a real person to compare ourselves to, we look to an ideal instead. We combine all of the best attributes we've ever thought of and paint an impossible picture of what we are "supposed" to be. Then, we compare ourselves to this perfect picture and sink deep into despair.

"Comparison is the thief of joy." –Theodore Roosevelt

We see what others are doing and mistakenly believe that's what we are supposed to do. And we are supposed to do it all. In just the right way. It's a big dose of harmful perfectionism sneaking in under the guise of a "noble cause."

- Always be organized, but never uptight.

- Prepare well-balanced, healthy meals, but stay within budget.

- Protect your child with your life, but don't be overbearing or bother other people about it.

- Don't yell at your kids—they will follow your example, so watch every step. (You'll likely ruin them if you mess this one up.)

- Don't let yourself go. Make sure you eat well, exercise, and look great. Take pride in how you look. But not too much… you really should put your kids first.

And one I'm sure we can all relate to...

Make sure your kid takes a coat to school when it's cold. They won't want to wear it, but you have to do your duty without a power struggle… firm, but kind… make it be their idea… reason with them, but make sure they know you are in charge.

I could fill the rest of this book with the (impossible) rules and expectations we have of ourselves, but I'm sure you get the idea. As funny as it is from afar, it's no joke when it's in our heads. And it *is* in our heads.

The List

When I talk with my clients who are struggling with feeling adequate in any area of their lives, it's really helpful to write down everything they expect of themselves. We get it all out on paper. I ask them a lot of questions and prod, "and... what else?" We keep going until we've got all those floating expectations out in the open.

When those expectations are in their heads, they seem reasonable. They even seem "noble" and worth criticizing themselves over when they fall short. But when we pull them out of their brains and put them on paper, we can see what's really happening in there.

On paper, it's clear that it's completely unrealistic for someone to do (and be) all of those things. It's not humanly possible to be the master of all things.

I dare you to grab a pen and paper and do this exercise right now. Write down all the things you expect yourself to do and be in order to fit your version of a "good mom." Keep going until you've listed at least 20 things (as many as 100 if you want). Go ahead, I'll wait right here....

Now tell me—what did you discover? Would you ever tell another woman that it was her job to do all of that? That's an interesting question to ask... do you expect of others what you expect of your-self? Or are you likely to cut them a little more slack and allow them to be human?

I too have high standards and strive for excellence, but unrealistic or perfectionist expectations are one of the most detrimental thoughts to our own personal progress. Sometimes, we are fooled into thinking that criticizing ourselves is "noble" because we believe our behavior should change, but negative self-talk and criticism are not the road to powerful positive change. In fact, in most cases, they will have the opposite impact, leading you to doubt your ability to grow and develop in the ways you consider important.

If you have a lot of critical thoughts, now's the time to use the work-book and see what's happening in that brain of yours. Let's get it out on paper and see what it's creating.

DO IT ALL AND INSECURITY

Jana hired me while expecting her first child. She wanted help adjusting to the new world that was coming her way. When her baby was born, she was going full force into making sure she did everything the best way she could. Inside, she felt a lot of fear that she wouldn't be a good mom. She was taking a lot of action to do everything "right" in order to compensate for the intense feelings of insecurity she was experiencing.

What I want to show you is that your insecurity can't really be cured by "doing it all," and in fact, it often leads to even more insecurity. Insecurity is a feeling, which means it's caused by your thoughts. So if you want to feel differently, you need to think differently. And thinking differently is completely available to you.

For Jana, she tried to compensate for her feelings of insecurity by becoming obsessed with cleaning and organizing. She wanted a perfect home to prove that she could be a good mom. Of course, she didn't realize this until we started checking in on her brain to find out why she was so stressed out.

She had a lot of thoughts that caused her to feel insecure. Not just as a new mom, but thoughts she had collected throughout her lifetime. Jana had the thought, "Something is wrong with me" so often over the years that it had become a belief. Now, as a new mom (which of course stirs up all of our insecurities), she couldn't stomach the idea that there was something wrong with her. It created a feeling of insecurity and new worry as she feared for what that would mean for her baby. After all, if there was something wrong with her, how could she be the mom her daughter needed?

And so cleaning and organizing became her way of proving to herself that she could be a good mom. Here's what her model looked like:

Circumstance: New mom.

Thought: Something is wrong with me.

Feeling: Afraid.

Action: Cleaning and organizing obsessively.

Result: Feeling anxious and worried most of the time.

This result reinforces the idea that there's something wrong with her.

Taking more action did not help Jana feel more secure. Sometimes, it would give her some temporary relief when she would pat herself on the back for a job well done, but that feeling would quickly disappear when things were out of order and her mother-in-law was at the front door. In the big scheme of things, it was giving her more stress and worry than anything.

> *"Perfectionism doesn't make you feel*
> *perfect. It makes you feel inadequate."*
> –Maria Shriver

So how can we go from feeling insecure to secure, especially when we are in new territory with a lot of questions?

Often, these kind of shifts are a gradual process. Jana could start with a thought like, "I'm learning how to be a mom." This thought may not cause her to feel instantly secure, but it does offer her some grace as she recognizes that she's figuring something out that she's never done before. It offers her reassurance that she's exactly where she is supposed to be. It puts her on the road to bigger and better things. Over time, practicing this line of thinking can have a massive impact on how we experience life and can free us from the "Mom Comparison" trap.

Circumstance: New mom.

Thought: I'm learning how to be a mom.

Feeling: Reassured.

Action: Taking positive action to figure things out.

Result: She is learning how to be a mom and improving.

Not only does this result prove that the original thought will surely come true, but you can see how over time, this model will create positive change. The more she approaches challenges from a peaceful place of seeking to learn and improve, she will consistently take positive action and eventually get to a place where she can feel more secure and more confident in her abilities.

Wherever you struggle with insecurity, you can use this same type of bridging thought. They aren't positive mantras, but rather thoughts that will serve as a bridge from your current thought to a more useful one that inspires positive action.

Besides bridging thoughts, another effective solution is to identify where you do feel secure. Remember in Chapter Two how we found ways that Jennifer was able to say no easily? It's the same idea here.

In our session, Jana and I were able to find plenty of things she was very confident about. She was particularly confident that she loved her daughter, and she believed that loving her was the most import-ant thing she could do as a parent. This might seem small, but if she was able to do what she believed to be most important, that's pretty significant. So that's what I challenged her to focus on. She would remind herself often, "I love my daughter unconditionally, and that's the most important thing."

When she remembered this, she felt hopeful about her abilities as a mom. She felt so much more empowered because she was confident that she was already doing the most important thing right.

When she was uncertain or doubtful and her familiar thought pat-tern, "I don't know what I'm doing" began, she was able to remind herself, "I love my daughter, and that's the most important thing." This thought always caused her to feel relief, and she was in a much better headspace to solve problems and figure things out. She was able to navigate through the unexpected with confidence and ease, knowing she could figure it out rather than making a mountain out of a molehill.

By creating a different feeling, she was able to create a different result. She didn't need to take action to change her feeling. She needed to take a look at her thinking and see what it was creating. Then, as she thought in new ways and created new feelings, she took different actions, which led to different results.

Yes, mom insecurity is normal, but it's optional. When it pops up once in a while as you practice these tools, you can recognize it for what it is—simply a feeling created by a thought you are having. You can remind yourself that you don't have to feel that way if you don't want to. You don't need to stay stuck in the "Mom Comparison" trap. There are always options about what you think, and you get to decide how you feel.

> *"Imperfections are not inadequacies; they are reminders that we're all in this together."* –Brené Brown

FEAR OF MISSING OUT

The fear of missing out is just another element of comparison and is also fueled by insecurity. We think we need to do it all in order to measure up, and missing out on anything might jeopardize our ability to do that. We all know what it's like to fear we are missing out on something a friend or a neighbor is doing, but it's much easier to handle that FOMO when it's about us. When it's about our kids, it's another story.

The best kids are playing on a select team—better sign my kids up too.

Every girl in the neighborhood has an American Girl doll—will my daughter feel left out?

All his friends are going to camp for spring break—I'll have to fit it in the budget.

We fall into believing that we need to do what everyone else is doing. We think we need to overextend our time and our budgets. Everyone is doing it, and we will surely miss out if we don't. And not just us, but our kids. Our kids will miss out! And of course, that means we are *failing* as parents.

Wow, see how quickly that went south? That's exactly what it looks like in our brains if we don't examine what's happening in there. The FOMO hits us right where it counts—our kids' success and happiness—and before we know it, we're certain their lives will be ruined if they miss anything.

Because of this, we end up making decisions based on fear rather than from a desire to create what's best for our kids and our families.

The big takeaway here is to recognize FOMO and call it what it is. When you're thinking of doing something or you are feeling anxious, find out if it's a fear of missing out. When you identify what's happening, it has so much less power over you. Suddenly, you can see what's happening in your brain, and you know that you don't need to make your decisions based on fear.

I always love to get input from someone who is outside of the situation to help me see it clearly. I never pick someone who is just as anxious about the topic as I am; that's a recipe for disaster because they will reinforce all of my fearful thoughts! I ask someone who's likely to see it as a neutral choice, so I can make a rational decision based on positive emotion. Try that when the FOMO rages and when you're feeling stuck in the "Mom Comparison" trap.

BRAIN TRICKS AND IDEAS TO CHANGE YOUR LIFE

You can see clearly that comparison, unrealistic expectations, "doing it all" to avoid insecurity, and FOMO are all adding a thick layer of stress to your life. The ironic thing is that while you're telling yourself that you need to be and do more, you're missing out on the joy that's available for you already.

There are plenty of ways to begin some brain shifting here, and you've already raised your awareness of the impossible "list." Let's dive into some easy ideas and things for you to think about.

How Do I Set a High Standard?

First, I'll address the achievers out there. There seems to be a misconception (and fear) that if you don't create a pressured environment full of comparison and a goal to "do it all," you won't be improving or setting a high standard for yourself. This is a lie.

I'm a huge advocate of striving for excellence. I think striving for excellence, when done from a place of desire rather than insecurity, feels amazing. I want to do my personal best. I want to feel good about who I am, and so do you.

I'm not suggesting you just ease up and live a life of mediocrity. I don't think that's much fun, personally. The problem is that if your personal improvements are driven from a place of negative emotion, you will always get a negative result. It might result in chronic anxiety, or it might result in repeated failed attempts to make improvements. Taking action from a place of negative emotion is the most ineffective way to move forward in life, and it feels terrible.

So, how do you have high aspirations without being so hard on yourself? Yes, you've guessed it—the key is in your thinking. Useful thinking will create positive feelings, which will drive positive actions and create positive results.

If you are stuck in the "Mom Comparison" trap and are setting an impossible standard, you are likely discouraged a lot of the time. If you believe you should "do it all," then you will feel like you are in an impossible situation. An impossible standard and comparison are the least effective (and the most unpleasant) ways to approach change.

"Understanding the difference between healthy striving and perfectionism is critical to laying down the shield and picking up your life. Research shows that perfectionism hampers success. In fact, it's often the path to depression, anxiety, addiction, and life paralysis." –Brené Brown

Let's say Kelly across the street is extremely organized. Organization and time management are challenging for you. You try to keep up, but you're not quite to her standard. When you overschedule yourself and miss an appointment, you immediately go to thoughts of comparison and failure.

Let's reference the thought model here:

Circumstance: Overscheduling your time and missing your appointment.

Thought: I'm such a mess; I can't keep up like Kelly does.

Feeling: Discouraged and agitated.

Action: Being irritable with kids, overeating, and ineffectively rushing to pull things together around the house.

Result: Worn out from constant stress. You don't feel good about the actions you have taken, and you're no closer to keeping up with things.

You have just reinforced the thought, "I'm such a mess; I can't keep up like Kelly."

When your go-to thoughts are comparison, failure, or inadequacy, you will only create more failure and inadequacy in your life. It's a cycle that traps you in feeling frustrated and never making the improvements you want to make. If you want a positive result, it will require useful thoughts that create positive feelings and drive positive actions. Those positive actions will create the positive results you really want.

Let's try it.

Circumstance: Overscheduling your time and missing your appointment.

Thought: I wonder how I can do better next time.

Feeling: Curious.

Action: Looking for for solutions and working to correct the problem.

Result: You are one step closer to being more organized. You've solved the inquiry of how you can do better next time.

Your result was positive and moved you closer to what you want. You were solution-minded rather than focusing on a problem or a perceived deficit. There was no need to compare and despair. You've also proven to yourself that you are perfectly capable of becoming more organized with your time.

Making Decisions YOU Feel Good About

Earlier in the chapter, we talked about "the list" of impossible standards. If you've already written your list, this is a good time to dive a little deeper. Once we've gotten the expectations out on paper, you can take the opportunity to connect with yourself and see what's really important to you on that list.

One of the reasons we stay trapped in "Mom Comparison" mode is because we make decisions about what we should do or who we should be based on everyone else's expectations and opinions of us. Growing up, we looked to our parents, teachers, and other mentors to learn what we should do. As adults navigating the unknown world of motherhood, we find ourselves in new territory and in need of guidance. We look to those around us to figure out what we should do, but oftentimes, we forget to ask ourselves.

Some of the most powerful work I do with my clients is helping them learn to live their lives and make their decisions by aligning more fully with their values. It's so empowering when we learn that our decisions don't need to be approved by anyone else. I can make decisions that I feel great about, and everyone around me can have any opinion (good or bad) that they want. It begins the process of letting go of fear of judgement from others.

> *"The more you love your decisions, the less you need others to love them."*
> –Unknown

So let's play with your list, you know, the one of everything you think you need to do and be to meet the ridiculously high standard you put on yourself when it comes to motherhood? Take out the list, and we're going to get smart about this by categorizing each item into one of three categories.

1. **Things that matter to you personally.** These are things that you highly value. Education, health and fitness, religious or spiritual teachings… anything could go here.

2. **Things that matter to others.** These are the things we believe we should do because we fear we may be judged by others. What on your list of expectations is there because other people think you should do it?

3. **Things I'm doing unconsciously without even evaluating.** These are things we do because somewhere along the way, we were programmed to just do, simply because we're supposed to. We don't see them as optional because we haven't taken the time to evaluate them.

Once you've categorized your list, you'll have a much clearer picture of what actually belongs on the list—the things that matter to you personally. With this new (shorter) list in front of you, you are closer to a more realistic picture of what to expect of yourself, no longer stuck in the "Mom Comparison" trap. This is when you can free up the time and energy spent on guilt and feelings of inadequacy and focus on actually becoming a better person. You can appreciate what you're doing well, work on what you want to improve, and *let go* of the rest.

"To be yourself in a world that is constantly trying to make you something else is the greatest accomplishment."
–Ralph Waldo Emerson

Questions

We've talked a lot about new thought patterns, and I've shown you several before and after CTFAR models. A great way to create new patterns of thought to get out of the comparison cycle (or any unwanted pattern of thought) is by asking questions.

You see, your brain loves to be efficient. It loves to answer questions. When you get an email with the subject line, "Can you answer this?" you immediately want to open it. You want to answer that question. It's an easy hook in marketing because it's such an immediate response in our brains, similar to wanting to finish a sentence by filling in the _____. (You said blank, right?)

Unfortunately, we usually ask ourselves terrible questions. We ask things like, "Why can't I figure this out?" or, "Why am I such a mess?" or, "Why don't my kids respect me?"

Why are these so terrible? Well... how do you feel when you ask them? Terrible, right?

What do these questions lead to? If my brain wants to answer a question, and I ask it, "Why can't I figure this out?" my brain will start searching for the answer. And the answer will look something like: "You are so undisciplined. You aren't smart enough. You haven't done enough."

I'm answering the question with not one but dozens of negative thoughts that are now swirling in my brain. Now I'm feeling inadequate, hopeless, and pretty much like a failure, all because of a terrible question.

With this example, it might seem that our brains' desire to answer questions is a curse. But trust me, the exact opposite is true.

If all I need to do is to ask my brain a question to create thoughts, then all I have to do is *ask the right questions*. If I ask myself, "What's perfect about this?" my brain starts looking for evidence that my current situation is perfect. It's like a teaser for my brain.

So instead of picking and practicing a thought, I can ask myself questions and let my brain automatically (the good kind of automatic) come up with one useful thought after another. When I allow my brain to do its job by asking the right questions, I've found a secret passageway into authentic thinking that creates powerful feelings, which will drive the kind of actions and results that I want.

I've outlined the process you can use to create your own powerful questions in the workbook. Go there to understand how to identify which questions are best for you personally. In the meantime, here are a few questions for you to try out.

- What is perfect about this?
- What can I learn from this?
- How can I do better next time?
- How can I create what I want?
- How can I make this more fun?

By asking the right kind of questions, you can pave the way for amazing new thought patterns. It's like an instant U-turn for your thoughts. It leads you to new ideas and inspiration. How do you know if it's the right kind of question? By noticing how you feel when you ask it. By finding out what kind of thoughts the question provides you. If it provides you with inspiration, ideas, and hope, it's probably exactly the right question for you.

THE BEST KIND OF COMPARISON

After all this talk of not comparing, I'm going to give you an exception.

"Comparison with myself brings improvement. Comparison with others brings discontent." –Betty Jamie Chung

I love to compare myself in a curious way to… myself. I like to pay attention to how I'm doing, what I can do better, and why it's important to me. In *The Practicing Mind: Developing Focus and Discipline in Your Life*, Tom Sterner talks about how difficult it is for us to be aware of our progress. We get used to a new normal, and we don't see the progress we have made.

Think about a kindergartner struggling to count. It might be hard for him. He tries and tries, but thinks he'll never figure it out. Fast forward to middle school. The child is now working on algebra and thinks he never makes any progress. He is completely blind to how far he has come. He looks at a kindergartner and says, "That's easy." But it wasn't always easy. He worked hard, learned, and grew, but he doesn't see it now that he's in middle school. He feels exactly the same way about his abilities now as he did in kindergarten because he has the same thoughts. He doesn't see the progress.

This is why it's so crucial to focus on your success and progress. We don't see our progress because we are inside it. Taking the time to look back and see how far we've come is a huge catapult for success. It will inspire hope and give you a sense of accomplishment. It's also a great way for us to get information. If I haven't progressed in an area I want to progress in, why not? What could I do differently to change that? When we drop the judgement and focus on the information we need to actually make a positive change—that's when the magic happens. So compare yourself to you. Compare with curiosity. Compare with compassion. Compare as a scientist interested in a solution. Compare with confidence that there is nothing you can't accomplish if you desire it.

THE RECAP

Comparing yourself to others or to an impossible standard is never useful. We usually compare ourselves and try to "do it all" because we fear that we don't measure up, but end up falling short of an impossible standard.

Falling into this trap will move you further away from being the person you really want to be. It creates feelings of inadequacy and failure and perpetuates negative thought patterns. In this trap, we are looking to everyone else to see if we are okay rather than looking within.

As you develop greater confidence and align with your own values, you'll be less likely to compare yourself to others. You'll compare yourself with *you* and create a life of constant personal development with internal fulfillment.

You can start by:

• Raising your awareness. Highlight the sections of this chapter that stood out to you. Reference them so that you can remember that comparison is simply a pattern that isn't useful for you. Remember that you are usually comparing yourself to a standard that is unrealistic. Continue to be aware of your thoughts of comparison and what they are creating.

- Implementing the solutions listed here:

  o Make "the list" so you can put down on paper the unrealistic expectations lurking in your mind.

  o FOMO: Call it what it is so it won't have quite so much power over you.

  o Use the workbook to identify thoughts that will help you set a high standard from a place of positive emotion.

  o Categorize "the list" so you can get clear on what you value vs. what others value.

  o Use the workbook to personalize powerful questions to inspire you.

  o Start the empowering practice of comparing yourself to *you*. Take the time to appreciate your progress. Focus on your sucess, and it will grow.

The Benefits

The freedom you will feel as you begin to climb out of this trap is empowering. The more capable and confident you feel as a mom, the more of a positive impact you'll have on your kids. When you make decisions that align with your values, you no longer need anyone else's approval.

P.S. You'll teach your kids how to make decisions from a place of integrity too. Pure magic.

To access the workbook, visit:

www.mollyclaire.com/HappyMomMindsetWorkbook

Trap 4

Making them happy: The Impossible Job

THE TRUTH:
You are designed for happiness, and no one can deny you that feeling. Your happiness is not dependent on anyone else or their actions. It's also not your job to make your kids happy. They are the ones that get to do that, and you can show them how. Happiness is your great privilege—I think you deserve it.

"Some pursue happiness, others create it." –Anonymous

THE TRAP: TRYING TO MAKE THEM HAPPY

As well-intentioned, loving parents, we easily fall into the trap of believing that we are responsible for our kids' happiness. You probably don't *think* you believe it's your job to make your kids happy, but traps are usually well-hidden. You probably think that you just "want" them to be happy. The thing is, there's a fine line between wanting their happiness and taking on the responsibility of ensuring that it happens.

Here's a chance for you to check yourself on this:

On a scale of 1-10, how frustrating is it for you when your kids are complaining?

How often do you feel guilty or annoyed when your kids tell you, "there's nothing to do?"

How often do you spend more money than you planned just to appease them?

(Starting to wonder if this trap has you completely stuck? Use the workbook to go deeper here. This is a *big* one, so please take the time to explore your thoughts there.)

Most of us don't like it when people around us are unhappy, especially our kids. We generally feel better when everyone is content. We may even have a sense of satisfaction that everything is going as it "should be" when kids are happy. I know I do. In contrast, when arguments and complaints come up, it feels like things are going all wrong.

This is what I mean when I say we believe our children's happiness is our responsibility, as if we can control the way they feel. We know we are falling into this *when we feel frustrated* that they aren't happy. If they are, then we can relax and know that "everything is okay." And here's the big one: if they are happy, we can feel better about how we're doing as moms.

While this seems like a pretty good idea, there is just one problem—it doesn't work.

You can't make them happy no matter what you do or how hard you try.

And by the way, it's nearly impossible to talk about this and not address the other key relationships in your life. This same trap causes enormous problems in marriages and strained relationships with parents or in-laws. We're going to start talking about how it's coming up for you as a mom, but we'll touch upon the others as well.

Why is this so important to understand?

Here's the truth as I know it: Your kids are going to be unhappy about half of the time. If you're trying to make them happy all the time, you are going to exhaust yourself. There's no reason for you to take all of that on. There is so much more freedom and happiness available to you as you learn and apply what I'm going to share with you and free yourself from this trap. On top of that, the more you let go of the responsibility of "making" them happy, the closer they will be to actually achieving their own true happiness.

This one shift can lessen power struggles, frustration, exhaustion, and your personal feelings of failure. And *this is not just about motherhood.* This is the key to greater happiness and fulfillment in your life. This is where it all happens. **This is the magic.**

YOUR KID'S HAPPINESS IS NOT YOUR JOB

Nope, it's not. Recognizing this is the most loving thing you can do. It doesn't mean, "I don't care if you're happy." And it's definitely not a pouty, adult tantrum that we throw in reaction to our kids when they are unhappy. You know what I'm talking about, right? Your kid is being impossible, and you say, "Well, it's not my job to make you happy. Sorry!" (But you're not sorry, you're just feeling terrible emotions and are throwing a tantrum of your own.)

Instead, I want to help you actually understand the fact that you cannot control the way your child feels.

Even if you wanted to, it's completely impossible.

Want proof?

Think back to a time that you bent over backwards to "make" someone happy. You went out of your way to accommodate or surprise someone, only to have little to no reaction from them. Or worse, if it was one of your kids, they may have actually complained about it because it wasn't what they wanted. As a mom, this happens on a regular basis. We do things our kids are "supposed" to appreciate…

and they don't. This is when you might mutter under your breath about how "impossible it is to make them happy."

And when you muttered those words, you were exactly right—It *is* impossible. The reason that your child is happy or unhappy is because of what they are thinking.

When I'm checking on my son's homework and keeping him on track, and he is resistant, I'm thinking, "He should be grateful that he has a mom who cares so much."

But he is probably thinking, "I'd rather be playing my guitar." Of course he'd rather play his guitar, and so he's thinking about the situation in a way that's causing him to feel unhappy.

The reason he is unhappy is because of his thoughts.

So if I can't control his emotions, I can try to control his thoughts, right?

We've all tried that too.

In this case, I believe he should be grateful, so I might try to convince him by giving him a lecture in the heat of the moment (because they always listen to those, right?) and shove a sense of gratitude down his throat.

While we can create *useful* opportunities to offer new perspective to our kids (not in the heat of the moment), it's important to first recognize that no matter what you do or what you say, you cannot control what anyone else is thinking or feeling.

If you're taking on this job of "making" your kids happy, you may even be venting that frustration to your kids. So now, your belief that you need to "make" your kids happy is creating contention and more upset, and as a result, they still aren't happy and neither are you.

If you've discovered by now that you've been attempting to master this task, you are not the woman for the job. You will never accomplish it, so please turn in your letter of resignation.

WHY ARE THEY UNHAPPY?

They Don't Know How to Manage Their Emotions

As adults, we are still learning how to create our own happiness and manage our emotions. It's what I'm teaching you here in this book, and a lot of it may be new to you. So if it's new (and challenging) for us, our kids certainly don't know how to do it. Why should they? How would they? They aren't emotionally ready to do that yet. They don't know how to manage their emotions and they likely believe that you are the one responsible for making them happy. After all, since you believe it, they believe it too.

We've taught them that it's our job to make them happy, but this is very bad news for them.

It might seem that our kids would want us to be responsible for "making" them happy, but actually, it's pretty frustrating for them. They already feel out of control of their emotional state a lot of the time. On top of that, if they think we are the ones who can make them happy, they have even less control over how they are feeling. And let's face it, a lot of the time we *don't* do what our kids believe we should do. You can imagine what it's like believing that someone else holds the key to making you happy… and yet they keep doing the exact opposite of what you want.

> *"Never put the key to your happiness in someone else's pocket."*
> –Anonymous

You'll probably discover as this chapter continues how you are putting your happiness in someone else's control too, and you'll recognize exactly how frustrating that is.

As long as you continue to take the job of trying to "make" your kids happy, they won't know that it's their job to step up to the plate. They won't even see it as an option. They won't understand that it's their responsibility and privilege to create happiness in their lives.

On the other hand, the more you model your own "emotional responsibility" (which we are going to talk about in a minute), the closer you'll be to teaching them how to do the same. Yes, as you focus on learning to create your happiness, they can follow your lead to create theirs.

We Are All Humans on Earth

We all experience positive and negative emotions—it is part of our human experience. We experience something, we think a certain way about it (both conscious and unconscious thoughts), and we create a feeling in our body. It was never intended for us to experience happiness and other positive emotions all the time. It was always intended that each of us would experience the full breadth of emotions.

> *"The word 'happiness' would lose its meaning were it not balanced by sadness."* –Carl Jung

The only reason it's hard for you when your kids are unhappy is because of what you are thinking. Remember when I mentioned the satisfaction you feel when everyone is content? And the sense that things are not right when there is contention or upset? This is only because you think your kids *should* be happy. Because you think that, you want to minimize negative emotions for them.

Circumstance: Child is unhappy.

Thought: He should be happy.

Feeling: Panic.

Action: Trying to "fix" his emotion.

Result: He's still unhappy, and you believe he shouldn't be.

With this result, you are still stuck with the same thought you started with.

However, you will be feeling completely different if you think differently about the situation. In fact, it's possible for you to feel contentment when your kids are angry, upset, or unhappy, especially if you believe that what they are experiencing is *exactly what they should be experiencing*. When we can accept what's happening as a natural part of life, it makes it so much easier to learn from it and move through it rather than fight against it.

Think about this... what would be different if:

- The best thing you could do for your kids is allow them to feel the way they want to feel?

And by doing this they could:

- Learn how to handle and process any emotions they experience?

And allowing them to own and experience their emotions will help them:

- Become emotionally healthy adults?

Would their emotional upsets seem different to you if all of this were true?

Michelle came to me for help managing stress as she was moving through some new territory in life. She had lupus and taking good care of herself was essential to managing the illness. Her 10-year-old son had also been recently diagnosed with an autoimmune illness. On top of that, they were preparing to move. Not only was she feeling worried about her own health and her son's, but she was especially concerned about the emotional well-being of her kids with the transition. She described her younger, eight-year-old son as highly sensitive and explained that her worry about moving was because *he* would be worried about moving. As she anticipated the move, she anticipated a lot of negative emotions for him, emotions she wanted to help him prevent. She asked me for advice on how she could help him.

You can see that the reason she was concerned is that she didn't believe it was okay for him to feel negative emotions. She saw it as a problem rather than something that's a natural part of life. (Please note, most of us *do* see it as a problem, because until now we haven't known any different.)

Not only did she believe that it was a problem for him to feel those emotions, but it was a problem that *she* was creating by deciding to move house when it wasn't necessary. No wonder she was feeling so much worry! As we examined her thoughts, we talked about what would happen if she continued her current line of thinking. Here's what we found:

Circumstance: Moving house and son is upset.

Thought: He shouldn't be unhappy and I'm the cause of this.

Feeling: Worry.

Action: Going overboard trying to reassure him.

Result: Making a mountain out of a molehill. He's more worried now because he's wondering if there is even more to be upset about than he thought.

You can see that if she continued to think, feel, and act this way, she would have created a bigger problem. She would have reinforced the idea that he shouldn't be feeling the way he is because his emotion wouldn't match the current situation. She would also prove to herself that she is the cause of the problem because her actions would have made a big deal out of a small challenge.

We talked about her beliefs around her responsibility over her kids' emotions. We also talked about the idea that kids, just like everyone, will feel a broad range of emotions as part of a normal human experience. And when we allow our kids to feel a full range of emotions without trying to change or stop them from feeling them, we are supporting their natural process of development.

Michelle had been feeling very tight inside with worry for her son before our call. When she embraced the idea that he was allowed to feel any way he wanted about the move, she felt so much freedom. She accepted his feelings and reactions as "normal" rather than a "problem" or an indicator that something was going wrong. This gave her the chance to be there for him in exactly the way he needed.

After our call, here's what happened:

Circumstance: Having a conversation with son about moving.

Thought: He's allowed to feel any way he wants to feel.

Feeling: Supportive.

Action: Listening and connecting without trying to change him.

Result: He moved through feeling some worry and came to a place of reassurance because he was allowed to feel the way he wanted to feel.

During their conversation, she allowed him to feel exactly how he wanted. She wasn't worried about his negative emotions this time, so she was able to just listen. Her calm and supportive demeanor allowed him the space he needed to process. By not trying to "fix" his emotions, he also learned that it's normal and okay to feel negative emotions sometimes. She was setting him up for emotional success in life.

A few things to remember:

- Kids are supposed to experience sadness, disappointment, and frustration.

- Kids will learn to handle emotions as they are allowed to feel them.

- When your kids are unhappy, nothing has gone wrong.

They Want to Get Their Way

I like to get my way; how about you? Kids are exactly the same, multiplied by about a million. When kids don't get their way, they will probably be unhappy. But remember, nothing has gone wrong.

> *"I've found what makes children happy doesn't always prepare them to be courageous, engaged adults."* –Brené Brown

Sharon is a mom of four, and she had a really hard time setting expectations and limits when it came to her kids. She was frustrated and felt guilty about not setting rules and following through. Rules definitely seemed to "make" her kids unhappy, and it felt like too much to handle. We did some work on protecting her time, but what it came down to was that she didn't like her kids to be unhappy. We talked a lot about why it was so hard for her and discovered that she felt an enormous amount of responsibility for ensuring that her kids turned out okay. So much so that it was suffocating. She felt like a constant failure and was worried about doing everything perfectly.

For Sharon, just understanding that it was completely normal for her kids to be unhappy about half the time made a big difference for her. She started to get used to the idea that allowing her kids to experience and work through negative emotions without interference from her was okay. When it was hard, she would reassure herself that this is exactly how it's supposed to be and nothing had gone wrong.

This was a powerful thought change for her. It allowed her to feel more freedom and happiness more often. It kept her from getting frustrated with her kids' bad moods. It also allowed her to follow through on protecting her time and taking better care of herself. As a result, she felt more like a person again, not just a mom.

Circumstance: Son is pouting and angry about a rule.

Thought: This is exactly how it's supposed to be, and nothing has gone wrong.

Feeling: Content.

Action: Continuing to set limits she feels good about in a loving way.

Result: Her son could feel how he wanted, and she stood up for what was best. It was exactly as it should be.

The "Moody" Child

Let's talk a minute about your "moody" child. I've got one, how about you? It might be particularly upsetting for you that one of your kids is unhappy a lot or extremely moody. If you have one like this, it's extremely helpful to look at your own thoughts about them and their moods to see if you are thinking in a useful way or not.

Here's what was happening for me with my "difficult" child:

Circumstance: Child I believe is "an emotional rollercoaster" is upset.

Thought: I don't know how to help him.

Feeling: Afraid.

Action: Reacting with impulse from fear; losing patience with him; desperate to "make" him feel better.

Result: Ineffective in helping him.

I've just proven my original thought that I don't know how to help him. This pattern is common for any challenges outside the norm, and it's so emotionally charged for us because we have so much doubt and fear around our own abilities. We have thoughts like, "Something is wrong with him," "When will this get better?" "I don't know what I'm doing," and, "I can't figure this out." But of course, these thoughts, and not our child's unique personality or needs, are causing the biggest problem.

There are several shifts that can help in this scenario, and I'll mention just a few. Simple curiosity can do wonders anytime we think we "don't know how" to do something. Asking, "I wonder how I can help him," brings a completely different mindset to the situation. It's also useful to remember what we talked about back in the "Mom Comparison" chapter. Remember, if you're exactly the right parent for your own child, then you must be fully capable of handling it. Finally, and perhaps the most useful thing, is just understanding and acknowledging that negative emotions are a part of life for them. I've already touched on this, but I'll say it again. Maybe when your child is a bit more moody than the rest, it's okay. Maybe nothing has gone wrong, and you can navigate their personality with ease and confidence knowing that you'll all figure it out.

THE ANSWER TO IT ALL: TAKE CHARGE OF YOUR HAPPINESS

So, now that we're clear that you can't make your kids happy, what will you do with all of your time?!

"Happiness is not something you postpone for the future, it's something you design for the present." –Jim Rohn

This is where we learn about shifting all of that "make them happy" energy to your own sense of well-being so you can achieve more of the good, peaceful feelings you desire. After all, you're reading *The Happy Mom Mindset*. Everything we've talked about really focuses on how you can be in the driver's seat of your own emotional experience and your life. When I talk about happiness, I'm not talking about just being happy in any given moment, but an overall sense of well-being in your life; the sense that you are creating what you want and are having a fulfilling experience throughout all the ups and downs of life. Happiness and well-being are really up to you.

We hear so much about finding someone to "make us happy." Relationship articles about "how to make him/her happy" are a dime a dozen. But the reality is that your kids, husband, and best friend can't make you happy. Only you can do that. They are an important part of your support circle and can add to your joy, but they cannot "make" you happy. This is really good news because if you are the one who creates your happiness, then you can do it any time, as much as you'd like.

This is where we are finally diving into the topic of *emotional responsibility*.

This shift changes my clients' relationships with everyone in their life. It changes their relationships with themselves. It changes their weight, their business, and the level of achievement they are able to reach. This concept helps them shift from feelings of failure and inadequacy to stepping into a place of confidence and peace.

Ready? Let's go.

Emotional Responsibility

"Happiness does not depend on what happens outside of you, but on what happens inside of you." –Harold B. Lee

There is never a time that you are not responsible for how you feel, because your thoughts create your feelings. Emotional responsibility is about acknowledging that you are the one creating the feelings you are experiencing.

In contrast, we are often taught to blame other people for the ways that we're feeling.

He made me mad. She hurt my feelings. They made me feel disrespected.

We've been taught our entire lives that other people are in charge of the way we feel. As a preschool teacher I would say, "Did Jenny hurt your feelings?" "Jenny, can you see that you hurt Jane's feelings?"

At a young age, I'm teaching Jenny that she has power over Jane, and I'm teaching Jane that Jenny gets to decide how she feels. In this scenario, Jane is powerless. She is at the mercy of what Jenny does or says in order to feel good about herself. And Jenny is proving over and over that she is not going to behave in a respectful way. So Jane is out of luck unless every teacher can micromanage Jenny's behavior.

The only reason Jane is upset is because of what Jane is thinking. Jane gets to decide what she thinks and believes.

Can you imagine raising this next generation as one that understands emotional responsibility?

So when Jenny says, "you're dumb," Jane gets to decide how she feels. She can decide if she agrees with Jenny's statement or not. Jane gets to be the one in the power position—power over herself and how she thinks and feels about who she is. Pretty soon, Jenny will realize that she doesn't have the control she hoped for. Jenny will have to face the unhappiness in herself and stop taking it out on others. It's a win on both ends.

I'm giving you this simple example because emotional blame has been all we've known our entire lives. From the beginning, in the movies and all around us, we are taught that everyone else is in charge of how we feel.

The truth is you get to think and feel exactly the way you want to feel. No one else needs to behave in a certain way so that you can feel good. This is amazing news! Few people in my life do what I think they should do. Especially my kids. To have the understanding and freedom to choose how I think and feel is liberating beyond belief.

Since this is a brand new concept to most adults, I'm going to break it down and look at some specific examples that may apply to you.

Emotional Responsibility and Kids

Just like you don't have the power to create feelings for your kids, your kids cannot create feelings for you. This is good news. While it's true that we can't really "blame" our kids for our feelings of frustration anymore, it's also true that our kids don't have to behave in any certain way in order for us to feel good.

So often as moms, we actually delegate our emotional life to our kids, and it looks something like this:

"Hey kiddo, you're five, moody, disobedient, messy, and needy… I'll put you in charge of how I'm feeling today."

"You, there, you're 15, insecure, hormonal, and entitled. Go ahead and decide how I'm going to be feeling."

It sounds absurd when you put it that way, but it's exactly what we do! I don't know about you, but I can't think of a worse person for the job. Would you ever consciously hand-select your kids to manage your emotional life? No thank you.

The only reason we do it is that we've had no idea we had choices up until now. We've been living under the belief that Jenny could hurt Jane's feelings, but now we know better. Now we know that we are the ones creating our feelings based on what we are thinking. Our kids can't make us feel anything.

The reason this matters so much when it comes to our kids is that our thoughts and feelings are creating results in our lives. And we want to create positive, powerful results.

A default thought for me is one that usually involves failure as a mom. Is it any wonder that I've devoted all this time and energy into helping you with motherhood? Yes, it's for you... and for *me*.

Here's what would happen:

Circumstance: My boys are fighting.

Thought: They shouldn't fight; I'm failing as a mom.

Feeling: Frustrated.

Action: Yelling at my kids.

Result: I don't feel good about my actions. I don't want them to fight, but now I've started a "fight" with them.

You can see that I've reinforced my idea that I'm failing as a mom. I've set up an impossible standard of success (i.e., "Succeeding as a mom means my kids never fight"), and I've also behaved in a way that doesn't get me any closer to teaching them good problem solving skills.

I blame my kids for "making me mad."

Notice what a powerless position I've put myself in. I'm counting on my kids' behavior in order to feel good. A lot of the time when we feel powerless, we try to exert power by getting angry and yelling, which ultimately makes us feel even more powerless because we feel emotionally out of control.

So, what am I suggesting? Am I suggesting that you simply "put on a happy face" when your kids are fighting? No. What I'm offering you is a self-reflection process that you can use daily in your life to create new thought patterns that create a different result for you.

Emotional Responsibility Is Not Self-Blame

Please do not mistake emotional responsibility for blaming yourself for the way you feel. When my clients first learn this concept, they sometimes move from blaming everyone else for how they are feeling to blaming themselves. They create a new negative cycle of feeling upset with themselves about the way they are thinking and feeling, but in reality, there is no need for blame.

Rather than blaming yourself when you have a negative emotion, you can acknowledge that you are the one creating it. You can allow it and notice what is happening.

You will create all kinds of emotions throughout your life. Sometimes, I create feelings of anger, sadness, or frustration. I don't need to judge myself for creating those, but I can understand and acknowledge that I'm creating them.

As a grown woman, Julie didn't have a good relationship with her mom. She desperately wanted one, but she said her mom always put her down when she was around. Her mother would say things that would "make" Julie feel bad about herself. What we discovered through our work together was that the reason she felt so bad about herself around her mom was because she thought, "My mom doesn't love me." This was a really painful thought for Julie. No wonder she felt so bad every time her mom made an unkind comment—it meant she wasn't loved, every time.

As Julie began to see that her mom didn't have the power to create those negative feelings for her, she started to feel empowered. She realized that she had the ability to choose what she believed about herself. But after a few weeks, she started to turn her thoughts on herself. She started to believe that when she felt bad, it was her own fault. She went from blaming her mom to blaming herself.

It's really important that I explain the difference between blaming yourself for your thoughts and feelings and taking responsibility for them. Acknowledging and taking responsibility for your thoughts/feelings is really empowering because it shows you that you are the one creating your experience. If I'm creating this one, then I can create a different one too.

Sometimes I create feelings of anger, and sometimes I create feelings of hurt. I know it's only because I'm interpreting the human experience and trying to make sense of it. I haven't done anything wrong; I'm just experiencing life. In my life, I will have day and night, light and dark, happy and sad, and every emotion in between.

Taking responsibility for my emotional life doesn't mean I "control" my feelings. It doesn't mean that I never think or feel negative things either. It simply means that I can understand what's happening and look at ways to create a different experience.

HOW TO START TO MAKE THE SHIFT

Whatever is happening around you is not causing you to feel anything. It's your thoughts about what's happening that leads you to feel the way you do. A friend of mine grew up in a large family. She saw fighting among her siblings all the time. She saw it as a normal part of life with kids. When she had her own family, she had a completely different perspective when her kids would fight than I did. She didn't consider their fighting to be proof that she was "failing" like I did. I'm going to show you her model with the exact same circumstance as my example from earlier in the chapter.

Circumstance: My boys are fighting.

Thought: This is what kids do; I can handle this.

Feeling: Confident.

Action: Redirecting or giving consequences in an effective way.

Result: She's handled it. After all, this is just what kids do.

With the same scenario, her experience was obviously drastically different than mine. Why? Her thoughts and beliefs about what to expect were completely different than mine.

Thoughts are the fork in the road. A situation doesn't need to be different in order for you to feel different. When you feel different, you will behave differently. Creating a shift to more useful thought patterns is the key.

As a coach, that's really what I help my clients do. We look at their current beliefs and thought patterns and see what they are creating. By making a shift at the deeper level, I can help them make changes that actually change their life. Think about it. I can try to coach someone to learn to control their temper, but if I can help them shift their perspective so they don't create feelings of anger so often, an even bigger change occurs.

You can call it seeing life through a new lens, a paradigm shift, or a new perspective, but whatever you call it, it's the ultimate change. It's how we learn to *think, feel,* and *be* happy, confident, inspired, empowered, and fulfilled.

Types of Thoughts

Let's talk about a few different types of thoughts and how you can begin to think about purpose. This requires you to first recognize what you're thinking now and second to understand the shift required to get the results you want.

Useful thoughts: *Thoughts that create a positive feeling, which drives the action required to get the result you want.*

We hear a lot about positive thoughts, but I'm more interested in useful thoughts.

I think of "positive thoughts" like fluffy thoughts. They seem great and happy, but they may not actually have any real impact on you.

For example, if I'm feeling like a failure as a mom and someone says to me, "You're a great mom," I might feel even worse. Because I don't believe what they're saying, I feel even more shame and guilt when they say it. Can you see how that's possible? Can you think of a time when someone tried to cheer you up with a "positive thought" or compliment that you didn't believe?

In contrast, a *useful* thought actually creates a positive feeling in you, which will drive a positive action and create a positive result.

A useful thought can be as simple as, "I care about being a good mom."

Ineffective thoughts: *Thoughts (often termed "negative") that create negative feelings for you.*

Sometimes, we beat ourselves up for having "negative" thoughts and get super self-critical about them. But most likely, the reason you are choosing ineffective thoughts is because it's simply a pattern for you. A pattern that we are working to change.

If you can think of them as ineffective thoughts, it takes away the element of judgement and criticism as if you are a negative person or are doing something wrong. They are simply thoughts that are not useful. They are ineffective in helping you reach your goals.

An ineffective thought will create a negative feeling, which will drive a negative action and create a negative result.

Bridging thoughts: *A thought that helps you transition into a better-feeling state. Bridging thoughts are also considered "useful thoughts" because they create the feelings/actions/results you want.*

Sometimes, the most useful thoughts are bridging thoughts. If I'm writing a book (right now…) and I lack confidence, then choosing the thought, "I know exactly how to write a book," may not be very useful for me because I don't believe it. In this case, I can choose some bridging thoughts to get me closer to the results I want. Some examples might be, "I'm learning to write a book," or, "I know some things about writing a book." These are things I believe to be true. These thoughts create a sense of calm confidence and allow me to keep moving forward with my book. They may not be bursting with positivity, but they are bridging the gap between where I am now and where I want to be. They are useful because they create the feelings I need to drive the actions that will create the results that I want.

Find Out What You're Thinking

You may be wondering how you can actually apply this to yourself. Of course when you're frustrated because your kid is failing math, you are not aware that you're thinking, "He'll never get a real job!" or, "I'm failing," or, "I should have done more." You just know that there is a problem, and you are having an emotional reaction to it.

So how do you know? How do you find out what's happening?

You ask yourself. *Without* judgement.

When I'm on the phone with my clients, I ask them questions to find out what they're thinking. I give them tools to examine their own thoughts as well. I'll give you some of the best tools and questions here that you can use to find out what's going on for you when it comes to your emotional life.

- Thought Download

  Write down all of your thoughts/feelings about the problem you're facing—the good, bad, and ugly. Offer yourself a place to spill your guts without judgement. This will get it off your chest and allow you to understand why you're so upset.

- What are you making it mean?

  When you are upset or worried, ask yourself, "What am I making this mean?" If your husband leaves a mess on the kitchen counter and you get mad, you might be making it mean, "He doesn't respect me." If your moody child is in a fit of rage, you might be making it mean that, "Something is wrong with him." Whatever you are "making it mean" is the thought causing a problem for you.

- Separate out the facts

  I've got some questions to help you with this in the workbook. They'll help you get clear about what's true and what isn't. The questions will guide you to see the difference between the facts about a situation and your thoughts about it.

- Use the CTFAR model

Use a piece of paper and write "CTFAR" down the side of the paper. Write down the circumstance and fill the rest in based on what you are thinking and feeling. This will help you get crystal clear about what your thoughts are creating. You will understand why you feel the way you do, and you will see what result it will create.

Questions to help you fill in the CTFAR model:

- How am I feeling?

- What am I thinking that's causing me to feel this way?

- When I feel _____, how does that make me want to react?

- If I take that action, what will likely happen?

THE RECAP

Trying to make (and keep) your kids happy is exhausting. You do it because you just want things to go smoothly, but we now know it's impossible. Besides, kids are supposed to feel unhappy sometimes—it's a normal part of life.

And the best news of all is that even when they are unhappy, you are allowed to feel any way you want; you are responsible for your own emotions! You can allow them to feel the way they want and focus on your own person feelings of peace, confidence, and achievement.

Emotional responsibility is the magic formula for a major paradigm shift that will change every aspect of your life for the better.

A few important things to remember:

- You create your feelings. No one else can create negative feelings for you. That's good news.

- Emotional responsibility is not self-blame. You create your feelings, and that's empowering. It's not a new way to beat up on yourself.

- Become aware of what kind of thoughts are useful to you by driving the feelings/actions/results that you want.

Find out what you're thinking by:

- Utilizing the Thought Download principle

- Asking yourself, "What are you making that mean?"

- Separating out the facts

- Using and filling out the CTFAR Model

The Benefits

The best part about this? Where do I begin???

When we are emotionally responsible, we understand that we are creating our current situations. By stepping into a place of emotional responsibility, you are claiming the ability to feel how you want to feel, do what you want to do, and create exactly what you want to create. You let go of trying to make your kids happy and stop the cycle of trying to make everyone else in your life happy too. They create their happiness, and you create yours.

To access the workbook, visit:

www.mollyclaire.com/HappyMomMindsetWorkbook

TRAP 5

MAKING THEM SUCCEED: THE GOAL YOU CAN'T ACHIEVE

THE TRUTH:
It's our great privilege: each and every one of us fails. We fail so that we may learn and ultimately succeed. You create your success, and everyone else (your kids included) creates theirs. Success must be achieved. It cannot be given.

> *"Success is achieved and maintained by those who try and keep trying."* –W. Clement Stone

THE TRAP: MAKING THEM SUCCEED

"Your child is so well behaved!" "She's so smart." "He's so talented."

Isn't it great when someone gives you a great compliment about your kids?

Or when you see them achieving great things?

You may feel proud, relieved, validated, and a million other positive emotions.

But what about when it's not such great news?

She got in trouble. He's failing math. She has a learning disability. He is autistic. She has an eating disorder.

The feeling is much different—worry, embarrassment, fear, devastation, or shame.

You probably have highly charged emotions on both sides of the coin. It's easy to feel relieved when things are going well and feel the weight of the world on your shoulders when things aren't going so well. There are a lot of thoughts behind these feelings, but one underlying issue is the belief or mindset that you are responsible for your kid's success.

It's easy to blur the line between being a teacher, guide, and mentor to your kids and being the one responsible for creating their success. We tend to buy into the belief that if we execute parenting perfectly, our kids will make the best choices and achieve the most success. We think if we live perfect lives, they will have perfect lives, and everything will be... perfect.

It's one lie mixed with another lie to make one big fat lie.

I bought into this lie hook, line, and sinker. Remember the idea in my head that my life would go from point A to point B in a straight-ish line? Yep, that's the lie. Right there. It's perfectionism, with a side of control, topped off with a big serving of frustration and disappointment.

Let's break this down. This big fat lie assumes that:

- You are supposed to be perfect.
- It's possible to be perfect.
- If you aren't perfect, your kids lives are ruined.
- You can control your kids' lives.
- It's better to control your kids than to allow them to learn how to make choices.

Can you see what's happening here in our brains? It seems like an honorable quest to live up to great expectations to ensure your kids' success, right? Except that it completely ignores the fact that you are human and your kids are too. They are given obstacles that are perfect for them. They get to struggle, they get to make choices, and they get to learn. They get to fail so that they can succeed. And their success won't look like the success of anyone else.

My three kids are completely different from each other. I swear my oldest child came into the world knowing how to be polite. I always felt a boost of confidence like a pat on the back when I would get rave reviews about his behavior. My dad would call him the "politically correct two-year-old" because he knew how to say things just the right way.

Wow, I must be doing something right!

Then… my second child came.

I repeated the same way of teaching him respect and manners. He also had his older brother saying please and thank you at every turn. And yet, his behavior looked nothing like his brother's.

What happened? I thought I had this down. I thought I was a mom who knew how to raise a respectful child.

I soon learned that child number two was not child number one.

I taught him the exact same thing, but his response was completely different. With such a specific issue and such a clear difference, I quickly realized that it wasn't about me, but about my son, who he was, his perception, thoughts and feelings, and how he chose to behave. It's much harder to see when the issue seems "bigger" or the stakes are higher. That's exactly why I brought up such a simple example.

The fascinating thing about this trap is that it's reinforced every time we take credit for our kids' success. It seems like a good idea to pat ourselves on the backs when our kids succeed, right? Well, I've found the exact opposite to be true. When I steal their success, I also have to steal their failures.

And the big problems with falling into this trap?

It's sucking the life out of every single one of us.

It's weighing us down and stressing us out.

It means that every time my kid makes a bad choice or doesn't meet a societal standard, I feel like a failure. Wow. That's a lot of failure if you ask me. Too much. Especially when you consider that every kid will do things like lie, avoid doing chores, complain, talk back, say mean things, get bad grades, lose a competition, and have no interest in following the rules sometimes.

If my success is tied to their behavior day in and day out, I'm going to be on a roller coaster of fear and failure.

We all have that fear that we're not enough, and this is one more way it manifests for us. I recently heard from a woman who said that what weighs on her the most is thinking that she's not doing enough as a mom. She told me that she has been a working mom and a stay-at-home mom, and in both cases, she constantly worried that she wasn't doing enough.

Clearly, it's her thoughts (and not her circumstances) causing her to feel the way she does. This thought pattern was one that she had no matter what her circumstances were. As you know by now, those thought patterns lead to feelings, actions, and results. When she thinks, "I'm not doing enough," she feels stressed out. When she feels stressed out, she is less present with her kids and spends more energy trying to do less-than-important things. As a result, she has proven the thought, "I'm not doing enough," and she still feels terrible.

When we believe that we are responsible for our kids' success, the "not doing enough" fear is magnified by about a million. Our fear is reinforced every time our kids make a less-than-fabulous choice. We use their behavior as evidence that we aren't doing enough. So if you've had enough of the "not doing enough" cycle, climbing out of this trap is a great step. As you get clear on the difference between your success and their success, you will have a whole new point of view.

Why will this make a difference?

Setting yourself free from this trap is an instant weight off your shoulders. Untangling yourself from your kids' success will help you step back and have a clear perspective on what's up to your kids when it comes to their lives and what's on you. You'll create more success as a parent because you'll be focusing on what you actually have control over: you. You'll also be closing the door on power struggles and frustration. You can get off the intense roller coaster of failure and realize that you're doing so much better than you think. Phew, that's what we all need! We are finally one step closer to the *Happy Mom Mindset* we're seeking.

This shift is exactly what Joanna was able to experience.

Joanna had a long-standing three-year math homework battle with her daughter, Catherine. You see, Joanna had fallen into the trap of believing she was responsible for her daughter's success and was frustrated as a result. After one coaching session of looking at her thought patterns, Joanna had such a drastic shift in her thinking that she was able to change the power struggle dynamic permanently, and the homework battle disappeared. She was able to support her daughter in a healthy way and allow her daughter to step into a place of creating her own success.

These are the kinds of shifts that are possible when we understand what's happening in our brains and what it's creating. This is how we go from stuck and frustrated to enlightened, empowered, and fulfilled. This is why it's so important. You deserve this kind of change too.

LET'S TALK ABOUT CONTROL

Fear is a huge driver of controlling behavior. When we believe we are responsible for our kids' success, we will experience frequent feelings of fear of failure. When we experience that fear, we tend to want to control things in order to mitigate that fear.

When my son started middle school, I could feel the panic rising in me. I had struggled in middle school as a kid and worried that I had passed on my worst tendencies—lack of organization and distracti-bility. I didn't see at the time what was happening to me, but I can see it now as clear as day. I was so worried that he would start to slip in school… and it would be all my fault. I didn't want him to experience the same negative emotions that I did when I believed I wasn't smart, capable, or good enough.

I believed his success was my success, and his failure would be *all my fault*.

Things started out amazingly well, and then, it happened. His grades started to slip, and he wasn't organized or motivated. I can't begin to describe the fear that I felt. I feared so much for his well-being and future, and I could not let this "failure" happen to him. I wanted to prevent him from this negative experience, and so I sprang into action.

My panic to "fix" this came across as pushy and controlling. The more I took over, the more I showed him how little confidence I had in him. I could be patient in helping him implement a solution… for about five seconds. But when he didn't follow through on an organi-zational system we had put in place, emotionally, I was back to square one with a driving desire to try to force him to fix this problem and succeed. This was more than just the issue of "manners" from when my kids were little. This felt like the big time. Not only that, but I was watching my own insecurity show up for him in his life. That's a hard pill to swallow.

Not only was I falling into the happiness trap by trying to help him avoid negative emotions, but I had taken on so much responsibility for his success that I'd left nothing there for him.

I was trying to shove success down his throat, not allowing any room for him to figure it out for himself. Here's what was happening:

Circumstance: Grades have dropped.

Thought: I've failed as a mom; I have to fix this.

Feeling: Fearful.

Action: Panicking and try to fix it for him; being pushy and anxious in my interactions with him.

Result: I've created a power struggle. He is even less motivated and feels like I'm trying to control him.

Of course, this result proves the original thought. Creating a power struggle does not align with what I see as "success" as a mom. I created the result by thinking, "I've failed as a mom; I have to fix this." I had the best of intentions. I wanted success for him. I wanted happiness. I wanted everything to be okay. But because of the way I was thinking, I was making it worse.

Does this sound familiar? How often do you have the best of intentions but end up yelling, controlling, or doing something else that you're totally embarrassed to admit? Yes, it happens to all of us. But *it's only because of what we are thinking*.

FEAR OF JUDGEMENT

We can't talk about this trap without talking about fear of judgement.

This trap is twofold; there is the part of us that actually worries we are failing as a mom, and then there's the part of us that fears that other people think we are failing.

Heather and I spent some time in her session talking about her son's electronic use. She worried that he was using it too much and didn't know how she should draw the line or set limits. As we talked, it became crystal clear that she actually had no problem with how and when he was using electronics. The only problem was that she wondered if other people had a different opinion about it.

We live in a time when there is so much information available at our fingertips about everything. As a result, sometimes we forget to access our own wisdom, our higher power, or trust our guts. We can get so caught up in what's popular that we forget that it doesn't really matter what's popular. All that matters is what we think. This relates directly back to the comparison trap and how we make decisions based on other people's opinions rather than our own.

"It's not your job to like me—it's mine." –Byron Katie

It's true that plenty of people will judge you according to your kids' behavior, good or bad. Judging is what we do; we are human. But you get to decide if their opinion matters more than yours or more than your own kid's well-being. How you feel about yourself and how you are doing is the most important thing. If you don't feel good about that… well, it just means we've got a little work to do in that brain of yours.

LET'S GET CLEAR ON SUCCESS

What is success? What does letting your child find their own success look like?

We usually think our child is succeeding (or we are succeeding) when:

- They have good behavior.
- They are getting good grades.
- They do their chores with a skip in their step (are you laughing or rolling your eyes?).
- They win. They are recognized. They look "presentable."
- They are "advanced" or talented.

Think about what you want and hope for your child… that's your version of success for them (and perhaps you).

So what does it look like when we let our kids own their success? We stop taking credit for it.

Are we really trying to *steal their success?* Of course not. We are trying to feel good about our own. The problem is *we blur the line between their success and ours.*

When you shift your mindset and let them own every success they create, it's quite magical. When your son wins the talent show or your daughter gets the honor roll, you can see it as their talent and hard work. It becomes all about them. You can feel lucky to be the one by their side. You can cheer them on and feel happy for the success they create.

The problem with feeling validated only when our kids do well is that it requires their cooperation and desire in order for you to feel validated. Let's face it—most of the work that we do as moms is never noticed by any other living soul. When we become needy and desperate for our kids to behave or achieve so that we can be assured and validated, it leaves us empty-handed most of the time.

It also puts us in that controlling, awful position of trying to shove success down our kid's throat. Even trying to make it impossible for them to fail. Impossible to fail? Is that really what we want to offer our kids?

We only do it in an attempt to diminish our own fears. But it just doesn't need to be that way.

The more you practice seeing their success as theirs, the more you can value and appreciate who they are as individuals. Allowing your kids to own their success is so empowering for them. It gives them control over what they create.

LET'S GET CLEAR ON FAILURE

What is failure to you?

Failure might be exactly the opposite of everything above—bad behavior, bad grades, losing, and not getting recognized.

We can also feel like a failure when our kids have a disability or a disorder of some kind. Not because they have failed, but because it isn't the success story we had hoped for, or we believe that their success cannot be what we hoped it could have been.

Just reading this might be painful for you. It's hard to see our kids experience failure or lack of success. It's even worse when we are mixing up their "failures" with ours.

So how do we let our kids own their failure? We stop taking credit for it.

Carol was feeling pretty desperate when she called me. Her daughter's behavior was "out of control," and she felt like no matter what she did to try to "make" her daughter happy, she was mean and refused to respect any rules. As we talked, it became clear that Carol was taking a lot of credit for her daughter's bad behavior, even completely blaming herself. The biggest problem for Carol was the thought, "I'm a crappy mom."

Yes, that was it. It wasn't her daughter's fits or defiance, but it was Carol's thoughts about them that were making her so upset.

Here's what was happening:

Circumstance: Daughter yells and throws a fit.

Thought: I'm a crappy mom.

Feeling: Hopeless.

Action: Parenting from a place of anger and frustration.

Result: Her behavior as a mom did not align with how she wanted to parent. She felt even more certain that she was a crappy mom.

Her result clearly proves the thought she is having.

By taking so much credit for her daughter's failure, she stayed in a place of self-blame that wasn't useful at all. She made her daughter's bad behavior mean that she was failing as a mom. Even if Carol wanted to be more effective and change her own behavior, she couldn't do it from a place of self-blame and constant feelings of failure. As long as she continued to think she's a "crappy mom," she would continue to create that exact result.

The first thing I did was describe to Carol this thought process and what it was creating for her. She immediately recognized that it wasn't the fits or defiance that were causing her to yell but the thought that she was a crappy mom. She could see that she was taking way too much credit for the behavior, and then, in turn, behaving in a way that reinforced that very idea that it was her fault.

Watch how this all changes when Carol stops taking credit for her daughter's "failure."

Circumstance: Daughter yells and throws a fit.

Thought: She's learning how to behave.

Feeling: Curious.

Action: Trying out a new strategy.

Result: She is one step closer to finding ways to help her daughter, reinforcing the idea that her daughter is merely learning how to behave.

You can see as plain as day that Carol's result was completely different with a new line of thinking. She didn't need to stoop to self-blame in order to create a positive result. By changing her thoughts about her daughter's behavior, she was changing her experience of her daughter's behavior and of course, created a drastically different result.

Not only does Carol feel better about herself and how she's showing up as a mom, but she's allowing her daughter the room to own her failures.

The more our kids can experience and learn from failures, the more success they can create.

"Failure is the opportunity to begin again more intelligently."

- Henry Ford

LET'S GET SPECIFIC... FAILURE AND RESILIENCE: THE MAGIC SAUCE

One of the biggest problems with failure is (you guessed it...) how we think about failure. Failure seems like a dirty word, and some people like to tip-toe around it or say we "haven't failed." But sometimes, I fail, and I'm okay with that. I see no need to avoid the word "failure," because I know the truth about failure.

Failure means I'm working toward something hard. It means I've got one more lesson under my belt in achieving the success I want. Failure is always an opportunity, so why would I try to hide it and pretend it's not there?

"Failure should be our teacher, not our undertaker. Failure is delay, not defeat. It is a temporary detour, not a dead end. Failure is something we can avoid by saying nothing, doing nothing, and being nothing."

- Denis Waitley

Failing only gets us into trouble when we make it mean that we *are* failures.

Can you see the difference between failing and being a failure? Failing means I made a mistake or I didn't quite get there. "I am a failure" is final. "I am a failure" requires us to quit and take up residence in our failed state.

Can you imagine how different life will be for your kids if they can see failure as an opportunity? If they can anticipate that it's part of the process and not a criticism of them as a person? What if they could understand that the only way to achieve the success they want is through a series of failures? Can you see that they would welcome failure and learn from it rather than hanging their heads in shame and hopelessness?

And it would be a million times easier for you to watch them experience failure too.

Yes, the reason it's so hard for us to watch our kids fail is because of our own thoughts about failure.

Take a look at the workbook to check your own perspective on failure. Your perspective on failure will have a direct impact on how difficult/ easy it is for you to watch your kids experience failure.

When it comes to your kids, you may have thoughts like:

Will he feel bad about himself?

I don't want her to be discouraged or sad.

I don't want her to think she isn't capable.

But failure cannot cause your kids to feel bad about themselves. Failure cannot cause your child to be discouraged or sad. Failure cannot cause your child to believe they are not capable.

The only thing that will create these feelings are your kids' *thoughts* about failure.

Lucky for your kids, you are beginning to understand that failure is really the pathway to success. You have the amazing opportunity to teach them a positive perspective on failure and model resilience in your own life as well.

Last summer, my son set up a conditioning regimen at the track. We were recording his times to compare day to day. One day, his time was slower than a couple of days earlier. He was discouraged and asked if we could just do the sprints without keeping a record.

He had thoughts about a slower time that caused him to feel discouraged. He was making a slower time mean something negative about himself. He was making it mean, "I'm not improving."

Here's what was happening for him:

Circumstance: Slower run time.

Thought: I'm not improving.

Feeling: Discouraged.

Action: Quit looking at his time record.

Result: He'll be less effective with improving because he won't have the data he needs to learn from.

We talked about the value of looking at the numbers and what he could learn from them. If he could see his times and how they changed over days or weeks, he could learn what exercises were most effective He could also see how his sleep or diet affected his speed or energy.

By being willing to look at his successes and failures and take full ownership of them, he was able to create more success.

He liked the idea of being curious about the information. When he was able to look at the data as information rather than making it mean something about him personally, it was much easier to use it to his benefit. In just a short conversation, he was eager to have the information, whatever it was. He was learning to see failure as information, which changed his perspective on it.

Circumstance: Slower run time.

Thought: I wonder what made the difference.

Feeling: Curious.

Action: Keeping a record and watching for changes.

Result: He is able to better understand what made the difference and achieve more success.

This ability to see achievement as a process requires resilience.

Resilience is huge indicator of success.

Creating more resilience in your own life is the perfect way to instill it in your kids. You can't fix your resilience by fixing your kids. Focus on your own thoughts and perspective, and you can send that outward. I'm giving you a sneak peak into the ultimate chapter coming soon, self-care; yes, it all starts with you!

WHAT'S YOUR RESPONSIBILITY?

Hopefully, you're already feeling more open to the idea that it's okay for your kids to experience failure, and perhaps you're beginning to understand that when they drop the ball, it's not all on you. Even the areas where you can improve can be looked at with a positive outcome, and there's no need for useless and discouraging self-blame.

So now let's talk about how you can get crystal clear on what's your responsibility and what's not. I've got some questions in the workbook for you to go through to help you differentiate between these two. You can take any situation with your kids that's leading you to feel frustrated or worried and do the thought work there. It will help you release control over things that aren't your responsibility and give you some clarity on where you really want to focus your energy.

Most moms have a hard time not taking ownership of their kid's success. Afterall, aren't they overseeing this whole growing up process?

I'm definitely not suggesting that you "let go" of your responsibilities or that you "shouldn't care" about your kid's success. You'll always care. And that's exactly why this is so important to understand. The truth is that you can't fail for them and you can't succeed for them. Success must be created; it cannot be given.

Your responsibility: *You are responsible for how you show up. You are responsible for the way you behave. You get to own how much you care, what you focus on, and what you teach your kids.*

Their responsibility: *Your kids are in charge of how they show up. They are responsible for the way they behave. They get to create success and they can own their failures too.*

Pretty straightforward, right?

Please don't confuse this for a lack of rules, limits, or consequences. Of course you'll do all of that parenting stuff. But if your kids break the rules, they get to own that and face the consequences. Just because you are doing your job doesn't mean they will always fall in line. Let's take a look at the example I introduced at the beginning of the chapter about teaching my kids manners when they were little.

I believed I had a responsibility to teach them manners. I did that job. I didn't do it perfectly, but I did the best I could. I made a sincere human effort to teach and to model. That's my part. The end.

I get to take 100% responsibility for how I show up as a parent. I can take 100% responsibility for my success and 100% responsibility for my failures. The more I take responsibility for my own actions—good or bad—the more opportunities I have to get even better. And the more I can look at where I want to improve with honesty rather than self-blame and guilt, the closer I get to being who I actually want to be.

Now let's look at my kid's responsibility.

My kid's responsibility was what they chose to do with what I taught them. Did they use manners? Did they listen? Did they forget? Sometimes they were polite, and sometimes they weren't. Either way, not my responsibility.

When we take responsibility for our kids' actions, we are living under the assumption that we can and should control their lives. It's like we are hijacking their experience of growing up just so we can make sure we will succeed as moms. But what if a part of your success is allowing them to make mistakes and being there for them as they suffer the consequences?

Even though the idea of separating responsibility is a simple concept, take a few minutes to do the questions in the workbook. You'll be amazed at how much clarity you'll have and how much relief you can feel when you realize that it's not up to you to "make" them successful.

MAKING THE SHIFT: WHAT'S POSSIBLE

I want to paint a picture for you of what's possible when you can allow your kids to own their successes and their failures.

Cara was beyond stressed about her son's SAT exam. He had taken a few rounds of it and was just trying to improve his score. She felt so much pressure to make sure she did everything she possibly could to help him succeed. Cara is an achiever and is extremely hard on herself when it comes to doing all she can for her kids.

She and I had our call while she was waiting for him to get home from school, and his test was the following day. She was in a panic. "What do I do? What should he eat? Do I force him to go to bed?" On and on the spinning went in her head. She was so worried about one misstep that would ruin everything.

As we began to talk about her concerns, it was clear that she was feeling responsible for her son's success and was moving into a place of feeling the need to control the situation. We spent some time separating out the facts so she could see clearly that she had done plenty to support him. We also took a look at her CTFAR model. She had so many fearful thoughts and, if left unchecked, they would cause her to make a big deal about the exam. She knew that the more she made it a big deal, the more nervous her son would get. Well-intended, as always, but her mindset of needing to control his success was having the exact opposite effect that she wanted.

As she was able to shift into a place of being clear and grounded, she could see that he was fully prepared to take the exam. He was responsible and did just fine managing his own sleep schedule. The more we talked, the calmer she felt, and she could see clearly that the best thing she could do was *nothing at all*.

She was able to see clearly what role she played in the process, and she felt pretty good about it. She was also able to see that he had to take it from here, and she didn't need to get involved. By recognizing all of this, she was able to be so much more supportive and actually instill confidence as she allowed him to own his successes and failures.

Just like Cara, when you fall into this trap, it's a very heavy and unnecessary weight on your shoulders, especially because it actually *requires you to try to control your kids*. The more you try to control them, the more out of control you will feel. We simply can't control what others do.

Let's talk a bit more about what can change if you shift your view on responsibility:

- You can be more effective.

When this heavy weight is lifted, you will be clear on what you can actually do to support your kids. You will experience less frustration and feel more in control of your piece of the puzzle. I didn't tell Cara what to do for her son; she knew instantly when her mind was clear of the unnecessary worry.

- Your kids will learn to make choices and take responsibility.

Kids learn so much from making choices. Whether their choices result in a success or a failure, when we take that opportunity away, we are denying them a very valuable learning opportunity.

- It will increase opportunities for success.

The more we allow our kids to own and learn from their failures, the more success they will be able to create. Failures are a necessary and powerful part of success.

- You can reduce your level of stress.

If my "job" is to make my kids successful, I've given myself an impossible task. And I get pretty frustrated when I'm supposed to do something but can't. When you focus on you and let them focus on them, you lose the stress and frustration created by your expectations.

- Get off the roller coaster of feeling like a failure.

Your success and how you feel isn't dependent on your kid's behavior or grades or anything else they do. When you stop tying your success to their behavior, you can see it for what it is. There is no need for self-blame or unproductive thoughts of failure.

THE RECAP

You cannot create success for your kids; only they can do that. They can (and will) succeed in a lot of ways even though you are imperfect, make mistakes, and totally drop the ball sometimes. When you make the shift and allow them to own their success, you put the power in their hands to create the life they want and simultaneously free yourself from this trap.

A few important things to remember:

- Your kids create their own success, and a "perfect" mom is not required for that.

- Their failure is not yours, its theirs. And it's okay.

- People learn, grow and achieve success by experiencing failure. Your kids are no exception.

The Benefits

The more your kids feel like they are in the driver's seat, the more motivated they will be to create their own success. They won't expect you to always pick up the pieces and make things happen for them. They will be on the road to independence, responsibility, and authentic success. They will take responsibility for their own lives at a young age.

And for you? This is the key to relieving so much of the pressure you feel. It will allow you to be even more supportive of your kids because you won't be worried about proving yourself. You can just focus on what's your part and love and support them through their challenges. You will feel confident and capable, which will give your kids exactly the strength they need behind them to make their lives amazing.

Less pressure, more success. Less contention, more connection. Yes, I think it's worth it.

To access the workbook, visit:

www.mollyclaire.com/HappyMomMindsetWorkbook

TRAP 6

A VICTIM OF MOTHERHOOD: THE REASON YOU FEEL STUCK

THE TRUTH:
As humans, we've been given the great gift of the ability to make choices. We get to choose how we think, what we believe, and what we create with our lives. Making and owning our choices means freedom!

"No matter what the situation, remind yourself, 'I have a choice.'" –Deepak Chopra

THE TRAP: A VICTIM OF MOTHERHOOD

Would it surprise you to know that it's really easy (and so common) for moms to get stuck in a victim mentality, and that this mentality is exactly the reason that so many women feel stuck, frustrated, and unappreciated when it comes to being a mom? If you're debating whether you should feel offended or curious right now, let's go with curious. As always, curiosity is where you'll find the solution you're looking for.

A victim mentality happens when we believe that everything is happening "to" us, and we fail to recognize that we have a choice. When our kids are whining and throwing a fit, we might think, "It's not fair," or, "Why is this happening to me?" When someone else's child seems "easier" than ours, we might think they are "lucky." This is just another way of believing we've been dealt an unfair hand. These kind of thoughts put you in a powerless position and cause you to feel self-pity and disempowered. And so we find trap number six—being a "Victim of Motherhood."

A few years ago in my coaching group, the victim mentality in motherhood played out right before our eyes. Erin had bent over backwards to plan a big trip to Disneyland with her first child and the proud new grandparents. It was really important to her, and she went to great lengths to get it all worked out.

If you've ever been to Disneyland with a toddler… you might know where this story is headed.

Halfway through the day, her son was tired and cranky. Erin was trying to manage his fits, but it wasn't working very well. No one else in her family seemed phased by the fits, but it was wearing her out. She was at her wit's end and headed back to the hotel with her son to try to settle him down.

She was so frustrated because she had taken the time to plan this trip and yet here she was cooped up in a dark hotel room. Why was she stuck with a crying baby while everyone else strolled through Disneyland eating churros? It wasn't fair. She was mad.

You may feel for Erin as you read this story. And by reading it, you can tell how frustrated she was. She felt that something terrible was being done to her, that she was being dealt an unfair hand, and that she didn't have a choice. This is a terrible feeling, and it was all created by her thoughts.

I remember the first time I found myself in a victim mentality regarding my kids. I was trying to sleep in on a Saturday (for the first time in months), and I had shut myself in a dark room on the top floor of our house. I was drifting in and out of sleep and kept dreaming that my kids were fighting and the house was chaotic. I soon realized that it wasn't a dream, and my kids were actually fighting. I was immediately irritated and started to get out of bed. "Why did this always happen? Why did I have to be the one to get up and take care of things? Why couldn't I just have one day to sleep in?" It wasn't fair.

Can you see it again in my example? I believe it's not fair. I'm blaming my kids for my unhappiness. I believe I have no choice but to get up, and *I'm mad*.

If you can relate to either of these stories, I've got good news for you. You probably fall into victim mentality sometimes, and that's the only reason you feel stuck and frustrated. Now that you know, you can change the way you are feeling by changing the way you think—and it's actually a pretty easy fix.

Why is this so important?

These may seem like normal reactions and frustrations, but the problem is that both Erin and I felt terrible. It might seem we are "allowed" to feel the way we did, and that's true too. The question is, is that how we really want to feel?

By taking a look at this pattern of thought, you'll see so many more options about how you experience what's happening for you as a mom. It's terrible to feel taken advantage of and disrespected, isn't it? The solution I have for you at the end of this chapter—yes, just one solution—is simple and can change everything for you.

What You Deserve

Even though Erin didn't like that she was so upset about the Disneyland experience, she had a hard time seeing how she could feel any differently than she did. It was hard for her to let go of what she was experiencing because she believed she *deserved* to feel angry and resentful.

Isn't it interesting to think about the idea that we believe we deserve to feel something so terrible? Erin's feelings were happening for her, not for her family. The feelings were in her body, in the hotel room, while her family was on Big Thunder Mountain experiencing none of those feelings at all. While she did behave in an unkind way toward them, she was the only one who was feeling terrible.

Another client of mine, Shannon, had a similar "I deserve it" block when it came to feeling angry and resentful about her husband. His long hours at work meant more work for her at home, and she felt overworked and underappreciated. She was too irritated to see any other options of how she could experience (or change) the situation. She believed she deserved to feel resentful, which kept her stuck.

As with Erin, if Shannon believes that she deserves to feel resentful, I'm not sure she's being so kind to herself. And she's certainly no closer to real solutions.

What do you think? If you are missing out on something that's important to you, do you also "deserve" to feel terrible? Or if you are working more than usual and you're tired, do you "deserve" to feel bad on top of that? Or do you perhaps deserve something better?

What if what you really deserve is to feel valued, loved and appreciated? I think that's exactly what you deserve. But you have to believe it in order to create that. And when you create that, suddenly you can see the real solutions that you couldn't see before.

What They Deserve

So what about Erin's family at Disneyland? Didn't they "deserve" for her to feel that way about them? And Shannon's husband? Isn't she just getting walked all over if she doesn't hang on to anger and resentment and try to force a change?

When we think, "It's not fair," we sometimes feel the need to try to punish whoever is doing this terrible thing to us, or we mistakenly believe that we can control someone else's behavior by feeling really negative emotions about them. Our brain tricks us into thinking that negative thoughts and feelings toward the offender is giving that person what they deserve or fixing the problem.

None of this is true—and as you're reading this, you can likely see it as plain as day. All that's happening is that Erin's family is still at

Disneyland, and she is not. And Shannon's husband still has the same schedule, but she's feeling worse by the day. The only thing changing for Shannon was a bigger build-up of negative thoughts in her head. She's getting further away from real solutions, yet ever aware of the vastness of the problem.

When we get caught up in what others "deserve," we close ourselves off to happiness and solutions. Besides, I don't like to live my life walking around as someone constantly punishing others for what I perceive they've done wrong. Not exactly the fast track to the happy mindset we are working toward.

If you're feeling stuck here, use the workbook to see what this "deserve" mentality is creating for you. It's easy to see that it's not helpful from a distance, but when it's our own life, it can be challenging to have the same level of clarity.

We all deserve to be happy.

The Thoughts and Feelings

Throughout the book, I've shown you a wide variety of thought patterns in different situations. The thoughts that go along with this trap are generally pretty standard. A victim mentality has a pretty narrow variety of thoughts, things like, "Why me? It's not fair. They can't do that to me. Why can't I have what I want?"

The common theme of these thoughts is that you have no power over how you are feeling. I had a client once ask me the difference between actually being a victim and having a victim mentality, but the reality is that both feel terrible. Our brain's interpretation of the situation is what causes all of the pain for us.

The pain we are talking about is the feelings we experience in this mentality. They are usually things like feeling taken advantage of, stuck, self-pity, disempowered, or even defensive. As you read this chapter and practice your CTFAR models in the workbook, find out what your pattern is. For me, it's a feeling of being stuck. When I believe something isn't fair or is being done to me, my victim mentality feeling is usually powerless and stuck.

For a lot of people, it's defensiveness, which makes sense considering we want to defend ourselves if we are being victimized, right? When you read the stories above, did you feel yourself wanting to defend Erin or Shannon in an attempt to defend yourself when you have similar thoughts and feelings?

Recognizing these thoughts and feelings matters a lot because it will clue you in to when you are falling into a victim mentality. When that's the problem, the solution is easy, and that's where we're headed now. Remember that when our way of thinking changes, our feelings change, our actions change, and ultimately, our results change. The best way to know how to change our action is to change our thinking first.

THE MAGICAL WORD (AND SOLUTION): CHOICE

You've probably noticed that I've used the word "choice" a few times here… that's because it's the key to getting out of this mentality. It's simple, magical, and it works—every time.

When it came to Erin feeling stuck with her feelings, the key for her complete mindshift was recognizing her choices and owning them. The truth was that Erin had made the choice to plan the trip. No one forced her to—it was something she wanted and chose to do. When it came to leaving the park, it was also something she chose to do. She could have asked her husband or one of the grandparents to leave the park. She could have called a babysitting service. She could have chosen to ignore the fits and noise. She could have left her son right there in the park with a stranger, right?

She could have done a lot of things, but the truth is that she wanted to leave the park. She wanted to go because she knew she was the best one to calm her son down. She wanted to leave because she didn't want to continue to try to manage the fits in the stroller at Disneyland. She wanted him to rest and feel better. She chose to leave the park because the other options were not acceptable to her.

As we challenged Erin on making one of these other choices, she was certain that she didn't want to do any of them. As she recognized and owned the choices she did make, she no longer felt stuck or resentful. She realized that she had done exactly what she had wanted to do. She could choose to feel angry about her choice, or she could choose to feel grateful, or peaceful, or however she wanted to feel. When Erin took full responsibility for her choices and her emotions, she felt a new sense of empowerment. She saw things in a whole new light with her personal shift—not something you can achieve by someone just telling you to "think positive" when you're upset, right? Erin went from feeling irritated and disappointed to proud and satisfied with the experience, and the circumstance didn't change at all.

This kind of shift requires us to be all grown up. It means that we quit pouting and blaming other people for the way we feel. This can be hard, but it means we get to feel how we want to feel, regardless of what anyone else does. It's magical and powerful to be able to decide how we feel.

I had a similar shift that day when I was hoping to sleep in. Fortunately for me, I knew exactly what was happening when I got irritated. I knew that I was creating it, and I knew why. I could see that I was stuck believing that I didn't have a choice but to get up and handle the chaos. I knew that in reality, that wasn't true. I went through the same process in my head that we had gone through with Erin as a group. What were my choices? I could continue to ignore the chaos and put earplugs in. I could drag my husband out of bed and yell at him to keep them quiet. I could lock my kids out of the house in the backyard. I could leave my house and go to a neighbor's or get a hotel room. I had a lot of choices.

When I looked at my choices, I immediately realized that I wanted to get up. I wanted to ensure they were getting their chores done and setting us up for an enjoyable weekend with a clean house. I wanted to manage the fighting in a positive way rather than ignoring it or yelling at them to be quiet. I had chosen to have these kids, and now I was choosing to get up because the benefits of that were more important to me in that moment than sleeping in.

This mindset shift created a completely different result for me. Instead of stomping downstairs and yelling with a "poor me" attitude, I felt totally at peace with my decision. I took charge in a positive way to let my kids know their behavior needed to change. I was able to bring an energy to the situation that totally transformed our day, and by the way—I felt fantastic.

Here's what would have happened with a victim mentality:

Circumstance: Kids are fighting.

Thought: It's not fair—I don't deserve this.

Feeling: Irritated.

Action: Yelling at my kids and throwing an adult tantrum.

Result: I feel terrible, my household has more contention, and I still believe it's not fair.

I would have created more of the very problem that I felt I didn't deserve in the first place. I would have created terrible feelings for myself and even more contention.

By recognizing my choices in that moment and making a choice that felt good to me, I completely changed the trajectory of my day.

Circumstance: Kids are fighting.

Thought: I want to set us up for success, so I'm choosing to get up.

Feeling: Empowered.

Action: Managing chores/arguments with emotional responsibility.

Result: Chores were handled, things calmed down, and we were set up for success that day physically and emotionally.

You can see that the circumstance was exactly the same, but the result was drastically different. The only difference was my line of thinking. The way I shifted that line of thinking was using that small trick of recognizing and owning my choices.

> *"Choice is what enables us to tell the world who we are and what we care about."* –Barry Schwartz

DROP "I HAVE TO"

So how do you use this magical solution? Exactly the same way Erin and I did.

First of all, I want you to understand that you never "have" to do anything. I don't have to pay my mortgage this month; no one can force me to do it. I want to pay it because I love my house, and I want to keep it. I want to maintain good credit. There are a lot of reasons I want to pay it, but no reason that I have to.

Think about the things you believe you "have to" do.

Feed the kids? Nope. Do the laundry? Not at all. Feed the dog? Think again.

These might be things you want to do because you want the reward for them. Or perhaps you really don't want to do them, and you prefer to find a different solution. Either way, recognizing that you don't "have to" do them is the first step in feeling and behaving differently.

I want you to challenge yourself today to drop the phrase, "I have to." It's never true, and it impedes your ability to recognize and make choices. This is what I did with Erika and her feed-the-dog dilemma.

Erika was another client suffering from the "it's not fair" victim mentality. Her kids begged her to get a dog, and she finally gave in. She made the rules clear about who would feed and walk the dog and when, but no one was respecting her rules. She told me that she "had to" be the one to pick up the slack. She was trying to drag her teenager out of bed early, and all the responsibility was falling on her.

Here's what was happening for her:

Circumstance: Family dog.

Thought: I have to pick up all the slack.

Feeling: Taken advantage of.

Action: Trying to force kids into doing their jobs, but she ends up stepping in.

Result: Her kids aren't doing their jobs, and she is doing it believing that she doesn't have a choice.

Can you see that the thought, "I have to pick up all the slack" is causing her to feel taken advantage of (and a bit stuck), and that it's *not* true? She doesn't have to pick up the slack at all. She has so many options, but she's so used to this line of thinking, she can't see them. It's also hard for her to see the solutions because she doesn't particularly like any of them. She's locked herself in to the best of the worst options and told herself she doesn't have a choice. Those choices that she's blocking out are exactly where her real solution lies. Her behavior of picking up the slack isn't the problem, and her kids aren't the problem—it's her line of thinking. Her thinking is driving the actions she's taking and contributing to a specific dynamic within the family.

Erika didn't have to feed the dog; in fact, she didn't even have to keep the dog. She didn't have to fight with her kids, and she didn't have to do anything else. As we dropped the "have to," she was able to begin to *recognize and own her choices*. And that's the next step.

3 STEPS TO FREEDOM

When you're feeling bogged down with "I have to" or thinking, "It's not fair," take the time to do three specific things. This is the process I went through on that Saturday morning, and it literally took me less than a minute.

1. Notice the choices you have.

Lay them all out! Think about all the choices, no matter how crazy they may seem. Yes, it is a choice to not pay your mortgage or to leave the house when your kids wake you up on Saturday. Look at those choices as real options, and see what goes along with them.

2. Decide what you want.

When you look at all of your choices and what goes along with them, it will probably be crystal clear what choice you want to make. The choice may not be "easy" or "fun," but that's different than making a choice you want to make. Paying the mortgage isn't "fun," but the benefits of doing it are exactly what I want. Make the choice and recognize it as such.

3. Own that choice like a boss.

I'm choosing to pay my mortgage because I love to be financially responsible and I love the benefits of having this house. I'm choosing to get up and be calm, cool, and collected on a Saturday morning. By the way, had I made a different choice that Saturday morning, I could have owned that too. I could have chosen to be angry and thrown an adult tantrum. I could have chosen to leave the house and given myself some space. No matter what your choice is, you can own it rather than blaming your emotions or behavior on anyone else.

For Erika and the dog, this process was magical. After dropping "I have to," we uncovered all of the choices she had. Erika had been blaming her kids for "having" to keep the dog and "having" to feed the dog, but she could now see that neither of these were true. She was choosing both of these things. When she stepped into a space of owning these choices, she could make a decision about whether or not she wanted to continue doing that. When she moved herself to a place of feeling empowered, she handled the situation in a totally different way. She decided she wanted to take care of the dog but would allow herself the option of making a different choice at any time. Here's what happened:

Circumstance: Family dog.

Thought: I'll take care of the dog as long as I'm willing.

Feeling: Empowered.

Action: Helping with the dog but being clearer with her kids about expectations.

Result: She felt good about the time she put in and about how she held her kids accountable too.

Our kids can spot a bluff a mile away. When she had threatened to get rid of the dog in the past, they knew she didn't mean it. She was thinking and behaving like a victim, which meant her kids continued to do whatever they chose with no consequences.

When Erika quit thinking and feeling like a victim, her kids realized that they couldn't take advantage of her. She changed her result and the dynamics in the house by owning her choices. Erika realized that by constantly getting after her kids, she wasn't standing up for herself at all. She was giving away all of her power and all of her emotions to her kids. Remember when we talked about delegating our emotional lives to our kids? That's exactly what she was doing. She was rendering herself powerless to their behavior. This was the ultimate shift in emotional responsibility for her, and you can replicate this same process.

THE RECAP

You always have a choice about what you do. If you believe you "have to" or "need to" do anything, it's a lie, and it takes away all of your power and ability to make choices.

Making choices is one of the greatest gifts we have. Don't you love to make choices? I do. I love to feel like I get to decide what I want in my life. When I throw the phrase, "I have to" at all the great choices I'm making, it completely ruins the fun.

If you sometimes fall into being a victim of motherhood, the simple shift of owning your choices is always available to you. The most common way to recognize when you are falling into it is if you feel stuck, get defensive, feel the need to blame, ask, "Why me?" or think it's unfair. These are clues that you are rendering yourself powerless and becoming a victim of your circumstances.

You can start with these tips:

- If you're caught up on what's "deserved," find out if staying stuck there is moving you toward positive solutions. Rather than what's deserved, think about what you want.

- Drop the phrase, "I have to," and always notice that everything you do is because you want to.

- Use the three-step process every time you feel stuck doing something.

  ○ Always notice the choices you have. Lay them all out no matter how extreme they may seem.

  ○ Decide what you want. Look at each choice and see what's the best for you.

  ○ Own your choice like a boss. Make that choice and remind yourself that it's totally up to you. Own the choice and all that goes with it.

The Benefits

Making this shift a constant practice will change your life. When you show up as someone who is the leader of their life and their choices, that's exactly how people will treat you. You'll shift into making choices you feel good about and you will feel totally in control of your own experience. As you become honest with yourself and your choices, you'll come closer and closer to making choices that align with who you are and what you want in life.

Oh, and by the way, you'll feel a million times better when you're no longer a victim.

To access the workbook, visit:

www.mollyclaire.com/HappyMomMindsetWorkbook

NO ONE IS TAKING CARE OF MOM: THE SELF-DESTRUCTIVE TRAP

T*his is nearly the end of the book, but **I hope this chapter is just the beginning for you**. Taking care of yourself, amazing care of yourself, is how you become a powerful force for good.*

THE TRUTH:

You've been entrusted with taking care of someone unique and full of potential and possibilities. It's you. You're the only one who can really make sure your needs are met and that you're well taken care of. Taking care of yourself is actually your responsibility. The challenge is learning how.

"The more you love yourself, the more love you have to give."
–Brooke Castillo

THE TRAP: NO ONE IS TAKING CARE OF YOU

This trap is the sneakiest of them all, if you ask me. It's disguised as being selfless, loving, and the most noble act of commitment and love. And yet, it has the most dire consequences. If no one is taking care of the caretaker… that's a big problem.

You may not have realized it, but *I've been teaching you how to step out of this trap since the beginning of the book*. We've talked about your time and how much you take on, and it's essential to understand this if you're going to take good care of yourself physically and reduce your emotional stress. We've taken a serious look at your thoughts and feelings to set you up to be mentally and emotionally healthy at a level you never knew existed before. We've discovered time and again the spiritual aspect of self-improvement—seeking inspiration and wisdom to fulfill your great purpose, find the answers you seek, and be at peace with who you are. Everything in this book points to becoming a healthier, happier, and more amazing version of you by taking good care of yourself physically, mentally, emotionally, and spiritually.

I've set the stage, and now… it's time to go deeper.

You are probably used to taking care of everyone else by now. It started on day one, back when Mom Autopilot was being constructed in your brain. It continued when you stayed up all night with your sick child in the hospital. Your kids' needs became the priority, and your schedule began to revolve around theirs.

And perhaps, *you started to believe that **you** no longer needed to be taken care of*.

It's easy to think that your needs or wants are no longer important; after all, no one else seems too concerned about them, right? And let's face it, you've got someone depending on you for everything, and this is no time to be thinking about yourself. Who has time to worry about you? You'll be fine, right?

Wrong.

I don't often tell people they're wrong, but I'm going to say it. Wrong.

Taking care of yourself, good care, even amazing care, is your responsibility. It shouldn't just be a priority, but your top priority (remember that priority list we made way back in Chapter 2? Feel free to go back and put self-care on the top of that list now).

We all know it conceptually. We understand that if we feel good, healthy, and strong, then we will be better moms, partners, and friends. But even though we know it, *we still don't do what we need to in order to make it happen.* My hope is that as you read this chapter, you will uncover what self-care actually looks like in your life and what it will mean for you and your future.

"Self-care is a divine responsibility." –Danielle LaPorte

Let's talk about an easy example, and if you've ever flown on a plane with kids, you will know exactly what I'm talking about.

On every flight, going anywhere, anytime, the flight attendants make a group announcement explaining how to use an oxygen mask. They make it explicitly clear that if you are traveling with a child or anyone else who needs assistance, you are supposed to *put on your own mask first* and then help those who need help.

Not only do they announce it to the group, but they go around individually to every parent or caregiver and tell them directly, *"Please put on your own mask first."* And just for good measure, it's also spelled out for everyone in the safety brochure: *put on your own mask first.* They go to great lengths to make sure we understand how important it is. Why? What's the big deal?

First, it will be instinctive for you to help your child first. It needs to be drilled into you so that you remember how important it is when that emergency happens. Second, it's pretty obvious that if you pass out from oxygen deprivation, you won't be able to help your child or anyone else. In an effort to rescue them, you will have rendered yourself incapable of doing anything to help anyone and will probably now require help from someone else. Can you imagine an inflight emergency where all of the moms on the plane are passed out? Talk about a flight attendant's worst nightmare!

Can you see how that happened? A well-intended selfless act ends up making it impossible for you to help and requires others to take care of you. Not very useful, if you ask me.

That's exactly what happened to me and dozens of other women I've watched suffer from unexplained chronic health issues or autoimmune diseases—migraine headaches, digestive nightmares, and major hormone imbalances. Not to mention the little things like being cranky, ineffective, increasing marital tension, and feeling pretty unhappy about life in general.

Diana came to me for help with her anxiety and tendency toward perfectionism. She was tired of worrying what other people thought and ready to move on from the spinning thoughts of worry she experienced regularly. Something Diana knew about herself was that she needed regular quiet downtime. She's easily overstimulated, and her mind races constantly. Having quiet time to decompress is essential to her well-being. The more she does it, the more grounded and energized she feels.

And yet, because she required more than other people around her, she questioned it. She even felt guilty for carving out that quiet time. She felt judged by extended family members for taking time to herself and told herself she "shouldn't" need it.

For Diana, this was one of the most important parts of her self-care plan. It didn't require a lot of money and it didn't require a drastic lifestyle change. It only required her to listen to her own needs, give herself permission, and make it a priority.

If Diana's child was easily over-stimulated, she would certainly teach him to decompress and carve out that time. She would put strategies in place to help him. But when it came to herself, it was hard for her to see that this was a reasonable and important step to better well-being.

This same principle applies to foods that your body likes, exercise your body craves, and joy your soul is begging you for. As we take a look at what self-care really means, you can evaluate your needs in a personal way. My self-care plan will look different than your self-care plan. Your physical, mental, emotional, and spiritual needs are different than mine.

Why am I teaching you this?

I don't want you passed out on the airplane while the flight attendant scrambles to rescue you.

If you've been fooled into believing that sacrificing your physical, mental, emotional, and spiritual health is an admirable thing to do, I want to help you take a look at what it's really creating for you. I know that as you learn to connect with, love, and care for yourself in a powerful way, you'll be the best version of yourself. When you feel healthy and happy, you can fulfill your divine purpose. When you are well taken care of, you are in the best possible position to care for others and make a difference in the world. I've met too many people who didn't learn to take genuinely good care of themselves until their bodies decided to rebel. They ignored toxic relationships, unprocessed emotional turmoil, negative self-beliefs, and physical signals their bodies were sending them. The truth is that they didn't even realize what was happening. It was easier to ignore the "check engine light" warnings and try to find a way around them, but eventually, the problems couldn't be ignored any longer.

You are too important to ignore the warnings. Your life is too important. I want to show you how to tune into your body and check in with yourself. I also want to show you how taking care of that amazing, unique, and gifted spirit—*you*—is one of the most important works you will do in your lifetime.

As you learn to put your oxygen mask on first, you can breathe and be invigorated. You can have more clarity and direction in your life. You can be exactly the woman you want to be, not only for you, but for your partner, your kids, and everyone else who matters most to you.

> *"How you treat yourself is how you are inviting the world to treat you."* –Unknown

YOUR #1 PRIORITY

Michelle was frustrated that her life was so busy. She believed there "wasn't enough time in the day" and wanted help prioritizing. She was tired of being tired and just wanted to feel better and actually enjoy her life! She had three kids and felt like she was always running around. She had a great husband and a great life, but she knew there had to be more to it than this constant "busyness."

We decided to look at priorities on our call together and discovered a lot.

Off the cuff, here are the priorities that she listed to me:

1. My husband

2. Teaching my kids well

3. My religion

4. Extracurricular activities for my kids

5. Exercise

Then we talked about how this priority list was working out.

Here's what she said:

1. By the time she had time with her husband, she was exhausted.

2. She did a pretty good job teaching her kids well, but the time she spent with her kids could be pretty wearing. She found that she would shut down sometimes because she was overwhelmed.

3. She was really involved with her church, but sometimes she just wanted a break.

4. The extracurricular activities were great! She felt good about what her kids were doing. But sometimes, she felt like they were too busy.

5. Exercise? Well, let's face it… this never quite happened. She was too tired to get up early, and by the end of the day, she was ready to relax.

You can see by this list that it begins and ends with exhaustion.

Convinced that she would benefit from taking better care of herself, I asked her a few more questions...

We talked about her sleep habits, diet, and meditation/relaxation. None of them were getting the attention they needed. It was easy for her to put them on the back burner and think they weren't important. Interestingly, she would never ignore those needs for her kids. It's just like the example of Diana, who would certainly help her son learn to create quiet time if that's what he needed, but felt guilty when she created it for herself.

We talked about the idea of making herself a priority, but it was hard for Michelle to imagine that. After all, there were so many people counting on her, and the days seemed too short. Michelle didn't see these activities in the perspective of "putting on her oxygen mask," so we decided to do some visualizing.

I asked her to imagine being well-rested, energized, and having mental clarity. What would her life be like if she felt *that* way every day?

Her voice changed immediately. "I would *enjoy* my kids! Our schedules wouldn't really be that hectic. Time with my husband would happen more regularly, and I really love to be with him."

It became clear immediately that her exhaustion, overwhelm, and lack of joy were a direct result of not taking care of her needs. As we took the time to imagine how different her life would be if she did take care of these needs, it became crystal clear to her what needed to change. If she was her own number one priority, she would be able to do exactly what she wanted in life in exactly the way she wanted to. All of her other priorities would fall into place if she started to take care of herself.

"Taking good care of you means the people in your life will receive the best of you rather than what's left of you."
–Carl Bryan

You'll remember from Chapter 2 that just because a priority is first doesn't mean it gets the most time; it simply means it gets enough time. It will get enough time so that everything else on the list can get enough time too.

Go ahead and take the time to think about it—what would your life be like if you were well taken care of physically and emotionally? How would you feel? How would you behave? How would you connect with your loved ones differently?

Understanding what's possible is the key to making positive change a priority.

SELFLESS OR SELF-DESTRUCTIVE?

"Caring for myself is not self-indulgence, it is self-preservation." –Audre Lorde

You're catching a glimpse by now, and you can definitely see how this level of self-care will help other women, but you may still feel slightly cautious about a "me first" approach. You may wonder if I really understand how much you value the idea of being selfless.

Let's talk about the difference between being selfless, self-sacrificing, and self-destructive.

I was taught my entire life to be selfless, and I want to be selfless. I love to make sure other people feel good, uplifted, and inspired. I love to help people. I love the golden rule: "Do unto others what you would have done unto you."

Which, by the way, is not a bad thing.

We learn to be selfless from our parents, our teachers, and our spiritual leaders. And it feels good. For the empath or caregiver, it's a no-brainer to put others' needs ahead of our own.

The problem comes when selfless becomes self-destructive.

When you became a mom, selflessness became a reality overnight.

Most of your decisions were about what your kids needed, and you were focused on a positive outcome for them. The desire to be selfless transformed into being self-sacrificing. And the trap we are talking about in this chapter is what happens when *self-sacrificing becomes a way of life that becomes self-destructive.*

Vickie came to me because she was completely overwhelmed with motherhood. She felt lost as a stay-at-home mom and told me that she never got a break. She had three kids under the age of four, including a six-month-old baby. She used to exercise, but not any more. She missed that rejuvenation, but with the breastfeeding schedule and her husband's long hours, there was never time for it.

She had constructed a belief system in her mind that her entire existence should be about taking care of her kids. Any time for herself felt like an indulgence. This line of thinking seemed so noble, but in truth, it was hurting the very people she hoped to serve. Vickie was falling into a depression, yelling at her kids, irritated with her husband, and living a pretty miserable existence. *It was the time of her life when she'd love to feel the most joy, but this trap was ruining her experience of motherhood.*

As with Michelle, Vickie and I spent some time visualizing what would be different if self-care was a number one priority for her. She could see clearly that some minor adjustments would help her fit in exercise. The benefits were so clear, and it didn't take much to make the changes, but the biggest challenge for her was the mindset shift that was required to make herself a number one priority. It went against everything she had been taught and believed. It required her to see the big picture and understand the benefits in order to make that leap into taking care of herself—amazing care of herself.

The way she was thinking about motherhood was creating her experience of motherhood. This was good news. By thinking differently, she felt differently, took different action, and created amazing results. As she started to make exercise a priority, she started to feel like a person again. She started to shift away from feeling irritated about her kids taking up all of her time and actually appreciated the time she gave to them.

Taking care of herself was one of the most loving and giving things she did for her family.

While Vickie's issue seems to be one of physical self-care, keep in mind there is a mental/emotional aspect as well. Vickie believing she isn't a big enough priority to get exercise is a mindset about herself and what she deserves. Her thought patterns about herself were causing her to feel unimportant and discouraged. That was the real problem. Lack of exercise was just a symptom of what was happening in her mind.

Circumstance: Three kids under the age of four.

Thought: I'm not a priority.

Feeling: Unimportant.

Action: Not taking care of herself.

Result: She isn't a priority.

She has proven her line of thinking and reinforced the idea that she shouldn't be a priority. If not interrupted, this cycle would continue to show up in other areas of her life. She would be unhappy, staying stuck and frustrated year after year. She would become more and more resentful of being "Mom."

Fortunately for Vickie, by seeing how important her well-being was, she made a mental shift that resulted in a physical shift.

Circumstance: Three kids under the age of four.

Thought: It's important to take care of myself.

Feeling: Valued.

Action: Changing the schedule to accommodate exercise.

Result: She is taking care of herself.

She is behaving differently, but she also feels different. Same circumstance, different way of thinking, totally different experience.

Now what? How do you do it? How do you change your beliefs about self-care and make this type of shift? As always, I'll show you.

KNOWING WHAT YOUR SELF-CARE PLAN LOOKS LIKE

You may be hoping I'm going to tell you now exactly what you need, but I'm not. I don't know what you need, but I know someone who does: *you*. By now, you've noticed the theme of this book—you are so much wiser, stronger, and more capable than you give yourself credit for. You know the answers, and you can do it. Any of it. All of it.

If you ask yourself what you need, you will find the answer.

Let's talk about the four key categories of self-care so you can take your temperature on how you're doing. I've got some questions here, and you can take a deeper look with the workbook.

It's hard to separate out physical, mental, emotional, and spiritual self-care because they are so interconnected. Some people believe that emotional and spiritual self-care are one in the same, but I choose to separate them. It's not so much "how" you categorize them, as long as you are giving yourself the care you need and deserve.

Physical self-care includes nutrition, exercise, and rest. If your physical health is out of balance, your other areas of life will be too. The opposite is also true—if you feel like an emotional roller coaster, you may end up eating your way through the pantry. These four areas will never be in perfect balance, but each day, week, and month, we can constantly tune into our needs and improve how we're doing.

Our bodies thrive when we exercise. The right foods will enliven, heal, and energize our bodies. Rest brings balance into our lives. These are essential components of living a vibrant life.

Good physical self-care is a gift you can give to yourself. I want you to stop thinking about food and exercise in terms of weight and size and start thinking of it as care and maintenance for your body. If you are exercising or dieting because you hate your body, you may be improving your physical health, but you are eroding your emotional and spiritual health.

Your body allows you to live each day. Are you thanking it?

What physical needs do you have that are not being met?

Do you move enough?

Is your body nourished and hydrated?

Do you rest enough?

What one change would make the biggest difference in your physical health?

Mental self-care includes learning and challenging your mind, creativity, and tuning into how your thoughts are affecting you emotionally. Continuing to challenge your mind is fulfilling because you are designed to grow and progress. The daily work on the home front is just about the most mindless work you can do, so as a mom, it's essential that you tune in to what your brain needs from you. Sometimes that need is even about quieting the mind too.

You can see that good mental self-care has a big impact on your emotional health, as well as the spiritual fulfillment you experience from growth as a person. We also know that physical exercise and nutrition facilitates good brain health and mental clarity. According to Harvard Medical School, exercise helps promote memory and thinking directly and indirectly. Not only does it have a chemical impact on the brain, but it improves mood and sleep and reduces stress, which results in better cognitive functioning.

There is no solid line separating any of these areas, which is why we're going to look at some key concepts to help you improve these different areas simultaneously.

Do you challenge your mind regularly?

Do you have a mindset of continued learning and growth?

Are you creative?

Are you aware of your thought patterns? (Hopefully, this is a YES by now.)

What one change would make the biggest difference in your mental health?

Emotional self-care includes social connections, relationships, and emotional responsibility. The tools in this book create a foundation for incredible emotional health. It's easy to think that someone else is in charge of making sure you're taken care of emotionally, but it's definitely up to you. That's good news, because you can make it happen.

When you are emotionally healthy, you're happier, and it's so much easier to take care of yourself physically too. You'll have that sense of balance inside, and therefore desire to create that balance on the outside aspects of your life as well.

As a coach, I have a coach and always will. It's easy for me to ignore my emotional self-care, but I've learned that it causes me to be physically sick when I do. Coaches, self-help books, or workshops are great ways to take good care of yourself emotionally. What might make the biggest difference is treating yourself the way you would treat your best friend or someone you've been asked to take care of.

Do you have bonds and connections within your community?

Do you have positive relationships?

What kind of energy do you invite and create in your life?

Do you create enough joy?

What one change would make the biggest difference in your emotional health?

Spiritual self-care includes your personal connection to your higher power and the connection you have with yourself. The relationship you have with yourself is spiritual in nature and includes the way you speak to yourself and what you believe about yourself too. Our greatest fear is that we aren't enough. How do you reconcile that personally and spiritually? How you relate to and understand your higher power will have a direct correlation to what you believe about yourself.

While self-talk has a mental and emotional component, it's a spiritual matter because you are a spiritual being. Connecting with yourself, who you are, and what's possible for you is a spiritual journey with depth and meaning.

Do you spend time soul-searching or connecting with your higher power?

Do you have kind and loving self-talk?

Do you connect with your own needs and treat yourself with respect?

Do you listen on a deep level to what you need in your life?

What one change would make the biggest difference in your spiritual health?

KEY CONCEPTS TO HELP YOU INTEGRATE BALANCED SELF-CARE

These four elements of self-care come together in some key concepts/practices that you can integrate into your life. As you work to improve your self-care, these concepts will help you get a full picture of how to take amazing care of yourself.

Connecting with Your Body

When you think about physical habits you want to implement, remember the importance of connecting with your body and tuning into your own needs. You may have heard about different food or exercise plans that work for different types of bodies. I've been fascinated to find that often the recommendations align exactly with what I've already discovered about my body by listening to it. Use whatever resources you'd like, or simply tune into what feels best to you.

Your body is one of your best teachers, but in order to learn from it, you need to listen.

My friend Katie's daughter is extremely picky and has a sensitive stomach. At the age of seven, she had pretty much put herself on a gluten-free diet simply from preference. Katie asked doctors repeatedly about it because it didn't seem normal. They assured her that there was no Celiac Disease or other issues that she needed to be worried about. As her daughter's stomach problems got worse, they pursued further testing and eventually confirmed that she does indeed have Celiac Disease. This little girl knew what felt right in her body, and she listened. She hadn't started ignoring what her body was telling her like most adults do. You can find the same things when it comes to your body regarding rest, foods, and the type/amount of exercise you do. The only reason it seems mysterious to us is that we don't connect with our bodies and listen.

Your body will also give you clues when your emotional life or relationships are harmful or out of balance. The Mayo Clinic identifies seven specific physical symptoms of stress on the body: headache, muscle tension or pain, chest pain, fatigue, change in sex drive, stomach upset, and sleep problems. In the western world, we find a medicine as quickly as possible to change these symptoms. It's much easier (in the short term) to ignore what our bodies are telling us. We want to eat what tastes good, do what seems fun, and turn a blind eye to problems that we don't want to deal with. The problem with that is we miss out on the messages our body is trying to send us. As we continue to take a look at self-care, think about how you can connect with and listen to your body a little more often.

Self-Talk: Your Relationship with You

How you talk to yourself everyday cultivates the type of relationship you have with yourself.

Think about a positive relationship in your life. It's likely that you support one another, listen and encourage each other, and look for the best in each other. You're willing to overlook their personality flaws, or at a minimum, you understand that flaws are part of being human.

Now, I want you to imagine what this relationship would be like if you were constantly criticizing that person and putting them down. Imagine talking to your friend all throughout the day like this: "Why did you do that?" "When will you get it together?" "Do you have any self-control at all?" "You might as well give up." "You're so weird."

"You don't fit in." "You're obnoxious." "You're boring." "You're fat." "You look so old." "You're not important; no one cares."

What would that relationship look like after a day like that? Probably non-existent. You would never speak to your closest friends like that, and yet too often, those are exactly the kind of things we say to ourselves day in and day out.

We are so unaware of how we talk to ourselves that it doesn't even occur to us that it might be a problem. Self-talk is thoughts. Remember, thoughts create feelings. If this is what my self-talk looks like, what kind of feelings do you think I'm creating? How do I feel about myself, and what kind of action will I probably take when I'm feeling that way about myself?

Circumstance: Getting together with a group.

Thought: I don't fit in.

Feeling: Timid.

Action: Not saying much; hiding.

Result: Not connecting with others and reinforcing the idea that I don't fit in.

You can do your own CTFAR model with any one of your negative self-talk comments and see what it's creating for you.

Make sure to use the workbook questions to identify your own self-talk. Take a minute to see how you are speaking to yourself and what it's creating. But be careful not to criticize yourself about criticizing yourself. For example, "Look how horribly I talk to myself... why do I do that?!" That's just continuing the pattern in a new way.

Self-Worth and Beliefs

What do you believe about yourself? What do you believe is possible for you? What do you believe about yourself in relation to others?

These are extremely revealing questions to help you find out if your beliefs about yourself are empowering or if they leave you feeling small and inadequate.

What you believe about yourself is based on programming over the years. Thoughts you've had about yourself over and over again have become your beliefs about yourself. What I love about the coaching model is that it focuses on creating new empowering beliefs about yourself by looking for and creating new evidence. The way you think and what you believe about yourself is exactly who you will become.

"You are what you believe yourself to be." –Paulo Coelho

Your self-beliefs seem set in stone, but they are not. They only seem concrete because you've believed them for so long. Loosening and dissolving negative self-beliefs is probably my favorite part of this work.

Any negative beliefs you have about yourself are optional. Growing up, you interpreted life through a child's eyes and created beliefs about who you are. Now you're all grown up, and you get to decide what's really true about you.

Gina was a client of mine who had some pretty negative self-beliefs. You'd never know it if you met her—she is a powerhouse in her business, and she exudes confidence. She is proud of what she has accomplished as an adult, but there was also part of her that felt shameful about who she had been as a child. She didn't think about it much but just tried to move forward, away from that person that she was. The work we did looked at why she felt all of that shame to begin with. She was able to see the younger version of herself through older, wiser adult eyes and began to feel proud of the person she had been.

Go ahead and take a look at the workbook to sort through your own beliefs about yourself. What do you believe about your past self? Your current self? Your future self? Explore this idea and see how it ties in with your big-picture spiritual beliefs. Are they in alignment?

Create Joy

Joy seems like icing on the cake that's "nice to have." Sometimes, we even think of joy as something that comes and goes, as if it just happens to us randomly. But did you know that creating joy in your life is kind of a big deal?

Joy is essential to a higher level of well-being, and it's an experience that you actually create. Learning to create internal joy will lead you to seek more opportunities for external joy as well.

"Joy is the best makeup." –Anne Lammot

When we are caught up in the "busyness" of mom life, it's easy for joy to slip away from us. Over and over again with my clients, I see this happen in a few ways:

1. We stop appreciating the joyful things in life we already have. Thought patterns creating pressure and worry keep us from noticing and experiencing the joy and gratitude available. We're so caught up in these debilitating emotions that we completely miss the miraculous and beautiful things and people around us everyday.

2. We have put ourselves so low on the list of priorities that engaging in joyful experiences no longer seems important. While we used to be engaged in life-giving activities and hobbies, we have now classified those as extras that happen if there's time (which there never is).

3. We stop thinking about the future. Growing up, we think a lot about our futures, and that type of growth and progress is deeply fulfilling. Once we "check the boxes" of adulthood, we just sort of coast. We feel stuck and bored because we now longer have dreams and aspirations. Your sense of self has been taken over by dull monotony.

Isn't it ironic that what could be the most joyful time in our lives ends up being the opposite? We're too burned out to appreciate and enjoy our kids, and before we know it, we hardly remember what the personal joys in life feel like.

You can take this concept a step further in the workbook on the "joy" pages.

Relationships

Positive relationships are vital to your well-being, affecting you emotionally and physically. According to *Psychology Today*, the quality of your relationships can be just as toxic to your health as fast food or environmental toxins. A toxic internal (emotional) environment can also lead to depression, stress, anxiety, and medical problems.

In fact, a long term study found that those in negative relationships were at a greater risk for heart problems, including fatal cardiac events, than those with positive relationships.

So what does this mean for you? Well, if you're taking good care of yourself, even amazing care of yourself, you may want to check in on your relationships too.

> *"Connection is the energy that is created between people when they feel seen, heard, and valued."* –Brené Brown

Emily came to me while going through the process of divorce. During her marriage, she had collected a lot of negative self-beliefs, and she felt pretty broken. Her husband of 17 years had cheated on her for most of those years. Even still, it was hard for her to justify getting out of the marriage. She had a really great outlook on life and tried to focus on the positive. She also had four kids who were counting on her, and she was really afraid to be alone.

The turning point for her was when I asked her if she would ever want this relationship for her daughter. Would she tell her daughter to stick around? The answer was *no*. When you shift your perspective and and see yourself as someone who needs to be taken care of, you can step into that role of caregiver, except this time, you're taking care of yourself.

Take your temperature on the relationships you have. It's likely that even as you read this, you have had a few relationships come to mind that you already know are out of balance. How can you ensure that you're taking good care of yourself and inviting positive relationships into your life?

THE RECAP

You've been given a unique responsibility to take extremely good care of yourself. You are the one to watch over, care for, and help through this life. Just like your kids have needs, so do you. If you ignore your own needs, you won't be in a position to help anyone else. If you're worn out and stressed out, you'll live your life giving the bare minimum because that's all you have.

It's up to you to make your own self-care your top priority. When you are filled up and cared for, you'll be able to offer the best of you rather than what's left of you. When you're energized and healthy, you'll have the energy you need to be at your best as a mom, partner, and friend.

Just because you're a mom doesn't mean your life is over! You can do things you want to do. You can create fun and joy. You can dream about what's next in your life and work toward making that dream a reality! Stay future-focused on the next big thing in your life so you can stay invigorated. There are a few big concepts you can understand and implement, including:

- Connecting with your body. Listen to your body and what it needs. There's no need to focus on what anyone else is doing or what they need. Tune in to you.

- Self-talk. Take note of how you talk to yourself, and take steps to improve.

- Self-worth and beliefs. What's the big picture of what you believe is possible for yourself? What you believe about yourself will always become true.

- Create joy. It's important to engage in soul-filling activities, have fun, create a feeling of gratitude, and think about what you'll create in your future.

- Relationships impact your physical, mental, emotional, and spiritual health. Create healthy ones, and be courageous enough to say no to those that are not good for you.

When you think about your own self-care, pick one area and ask yourself what needs to change. Pick one thing, and make it happen. Meaningful change happens when small things are done consistently over time. You can take a look at your physical, emotional, mental, and spiritual needs and ask yourself if they are being met. Where could you improve, and how will that impact you?

The Benefits

Taking good care of yourself feels amazing! It's the pathway to vibrancy and longevity. Besides, it feels good to remember that you're important. It's nice to know someone is looking after you and taking care of you. When you give yourself that gift, it keeps on giving. You'll feel better about yourself and more loving toward your kids, your partner, and all your loved ones. You'll be less grouchy and irritable and find a little more joy in the meaningless and mundane tasks that used to annoy you. Your well-being is about so much more than exercise and diet. You deserve to feel well physically, emotionally, mentally, and spiritually.

This is truly the key to freeing yourself from the traps of motherhood: remember that you are important, that your body, mind, and soul deserve to be cared for, and you still get to lead a life that excites you!

To access the workbook, visit:

www.mollyclaire.com/HappyMomMindsetWorkbook.

CONCLUSION

BRINGING IT ALL TOGETHER, BELIEFS, AND MOVING FORWARD

"Your present circumstances don't determine where you can go, they merely determine where you start." —Nido Qubein

I hope you've enjoyed this book as much as I've enjoyed writing it. And when I say that I enjoyed writing it, I mean that sometimes I wanted to hide from my computer and quit completely. I questioned myself and wondered if anyone would learn anything from it. It took much longer than I thought it would. I felt frustration, doubt, and was completely stuck sometimes.

Other times, I felt inspired and connected to you even though we've never met. I felt joy and fulfillment as I thought about how you might be able to use these tools. I felt called to write this book, and I knew I couldn't escape it no matter how hard it was. Fulfilling this purpose was my great desire, no matter how challenging the road.

Just like motherhood.

Yes, that's right—we've come full circle to the unexpected that is ever-present in motherhood and all of the other most meaningful experiences of our lives. The line from point A to point B is never straight, but it's always meaningful.

The "Happy Mom Mindset" is all about stepping into a place of creating joy and meaningful experiences along the way. It's about understanding that within your circumstances is your internal experience that's completely up to you. What you create within will manifest externally in your life as well.

BEYOND MOTHERHOOD: POWERFUL BELIEFS FOR LIFE

Each chapter, each trap, has taught you about ways you can have a better experience of motherhood, but with these tools, you can do so much more. You can use these concepts to do the exact same thing in all areas of your life. Your mind and intentions are the key to creating exactly what you want.

I'm going to share with you some of my favorite beliefs that impact my life every day. I've also got some guidance for you in the workbook to come up with your own. Powerful beliefs create a powerful life.

This is exactly how it's supposed to be.

Whatever is happening is supposed to be happening. Sometimes, we argue with reality, and when we believe things should be different than they are, it's really frustrating. I always try to remember that what is happening is supposed to happen. It helps me accept what is with peace while becoming more aware of what I actually have a say in.

"Suffering is arguing with reality." –Byron Katie

"Be still and know that I am God." –Psalm 46:10

"God grant me the serenity to accept the things I cannot change, courage to change the things I can, and wisdom to know the difference." –The Serenity Prayer

There is always plenty of time to do exactly what I need to do.

When you believe there's never enough time, you will always create that result. When you believe there is plenty of time, you become a problem solver, making the things that really matter happen. This belief will allow you to enjoy the present moment and be wise with your time in a fulfilling way. I love the belief and what it creates for me.

"Time has a wonderful way of showing us what really matters." –Margaret Peters

"In time, things will fall right in place." –Unknown

"The present moment is the only moment available to us, and it is the door to all moments." –Thich Nhat Hanh

Love is always available

Feeling love for someone is always available to you. You don't need to love what someone does in order to feel love for them. When I give myself permission to love everyone no matter what, it's amazing.

"But love ye your enemies, and do good, and lend, hoping for nothing again; and your reward shall be great..." –Luke 6:35

"Give love and unconditional acceptance to those you encounter, and notice what happens." –Wayne Dyer

I am meant to succeed.

It doesn't matter how many times you "fail," because ultimately, you are meant to succeed. You are designed to grow, become, and succeed in a huge way—it's always been in the plan for you.

"The temptation to quit will be greatest just before you are about to succeed." –Chinese Proverb

"Rise up and become the person you were meant to be."
–Dieter F. Uchtdorf

"Do you have the courage to bring forth the treasures that are hidden within you?" –Elizabeth Gilbert

The universe is always conspiring for me

When I know that everything is happening for me, I learn from every moment of my life. I rarely feel discouraged, because I know that something great is just around the corner. I feel the power of something bigger than me cheering me on and putting exactly what I need in my path. It's not me against the world; it's the universe behind me 100%.

"If you have God on your side, everything becomes clear."
–Ayrton Senna

"Life is simple. Everything happens for you, not to you. Everything happens at exactly the right moment, neither too soon nor too late." –Byron Katie

I can always create what I want

My circumstances never stop me from creating what I want when I remember that whatever I want is always an option. I love to ask myself how I can create what I want when things don't seem be be lining up for me. This question always shows me what steps to take to create an internal and external experience—that's just what I want.

"The desire to create is one of the deepest yearnings of the soul." –Dieter F. Uchtdorf

"Life is what you make it. Always has been, always will be."
–Eleanor Roosevelt

MOVING FORWARD

I want to send you off in exactly the way we met, by reminding you of how amazing and powerful you are.

And remember, this isn't the end. It's really a new beginning for you.

You have taken on a task that requires all of you. It requires your heart and soul. It requires you to face your deepest fears of inadequacy and walk through rough terrain that often seems impossible. It requires you to be vulnerable, worried, and completely overwhelmed (sometimes all at the same time).

But you said yes. And you keep at it every day.

Who you are you makes you uniquely qualified to live your life and be the woman to raise your kids. What you do every day matters so much. Even when no one notices, and no one is thankful, it matters.

The mistakes you make will be forgotten, but the lessons you teach will be remembered.

You were never supposed to be perfect. You're doing exactly what you're supposed to do as best as you can with what you have in this moment. That's how mistakes and successes are made.

Please be your own best friend.

Be your biggest supporter, especially when you're down. That's when you need support the most. Give it to yourself in the biggest way. Remember to reach out to others and create your own support system. You're doing hard work, so please create a team to rally around you, love you, and believe in you.

Your future will happen. It can happen to you, or you can create it. You get to decide.

The circumstances in your life don't have to limit where you go, what you create, or who you become. They are simply a starting point.

Your life awaits. What will you do with it?

I can't wait to find out.

Dear Reader,

I hope you've enjoyed our time together. This work changed my life, and it can change yours too.

Above all, remember to listen to what speaks to you here. And if you're being nudged to take it all further, listen to that nudge.

Investing in yourself usually requires a leap of faith and a healthy dose of courage. It requires you to believe that a little more is possible for your life. If the desire for change is stirring in you now, come with me.

This book wasn't just produced for the masses; it was written with you in mind. It's for the one. It's for you. And my work is for you too.

If you want more information on the latest programs, groups, and retreats, come see me at www.mollyclaire.com and subscribe to my list. There's always something new happening, and I'd love to have you join me.

Until then, take good care of yourself, one thought at a time…

I'll see you soon.

Molly

References

The 7 Habits of Highly Effective People by Stephen R. Covey

"Regular exercise changes the brain to improve memory, thinking skills" by Heidi Godman from *Harvard Health Letter*

"Stress symptoms: Effects on your body and behavior" by the Mayo Clinic Staff from the Mayo Clinic

"The Hidden Health Hazards of Toxic Relationships" by Sherrie Bourg Carter Psy.D. from *Psychology Today*

The Practicing Mind: Developing Focus and Discipline in Your Life — Master Any Skill or Challenge by Learning to Love the Process by Thomas Sterner

ABOUT THE AUTHOR

Molly Claire is a Master Certified Life Coach who is passionate about helping her clients achieve their greatest potential. Molly speaks, teaches, and coaches women from around the world and believes that as individuals change, so does the world.

Her business is merely an extension of how she feels about raising her kids—helping each of them to become who they are meant to be and create a fulfilling life. She is honored to have the opportunity to support women who make such a difference every day.

Molly has always had a keen interest in brain development, specifically in early childhood. During her years as a stay-at-home mom, she created preschool groups and taught at a private preschool, always implementing strategies to encourage healthy brain development.

When Molly found life coaching, she was amazed at how the cognitive process helped her change her life. That's when she knew that she wanted to help other women understand their brain as well and understand (and change) their lives.

Molly is double certified as a Master Life and Weight Loss Coach. She also trains coaches for The Life Coach School and walks with them side by side as they complete the certification process.

Molly is the proud mom of a musician, an athlete, and a strong-willed bundle of "sugar and spice" (heavy on the spice). They are her pride and joy. They challenge her daily and are her greatest teachers.

Molly Claire offers private and group coaching by phone, online, and through live retreats. Visit Molly's website at www.mollyclaire.com for free resources and to learn about *The Happy Mom Mindset* program, coaching, and podcast.

Made in the USA
San Bernardino, CA
03 May 2018